PENGUIN
STUDIO

Photographs by

COURTNEY MILNE

VISIONS

of the

GODDESS

Text by Sherrill Miller

PENGUIN
STUDIO

PENGUIN STUDIO

Published by the Penguin Group

Penguin Books Canada Ltd, 10 Alcorn Avenue, Toronto, Ontario, Canada M4V 3B2

Penguin Books Ltd, 27 Wrights Lane London, W8 5TZ, England

Penguin Putnam Inc., 375 Hudson Street, New York, New York 10014, USA

Penguin Books Australia Ltd, Ringwood, Victoria, Australia

Penguin Books (NZ) Ltd, cnr Rosedale and Airborne Roads, Albany, Auckland 1310, New Zealand

Penguin Books Ltd, Registered Offices: Harmondsworth, Middlesex, England

First published 1998

10 9 8 7 6 5 4 3 2 1

Photographs copyright © Courtney Milne, 1998

Text copyright © Sherrill Miller, 1998

Printed and bound in Singapore on acid free paper

Design and page production by Counterpunch

Canadian Cataloguing in Publication Data

Milne, Courtney, 1943 –

    Visions of the Goddess

ISBN 0-670-87439-6

1. Goddess.   2. Goddess – Pictorial works.   I. Miller, Sherrill, 1946–   II. Title

BL473.5M54 1998   291.2'114'0222   C97-932753-9

American Library of Congress Cataloguing in Publication Data Available

Visit Penguin Canada's web site at www.penguin.ca

PHOTO PAGE 2: *Dawn light on Pacific Ocean, Fraser Island, Australia, 1989.*

PHOTO PAGE 3: *Sand dunes, Namib-Nauklift Park, Namibia, 1994.*

Contents

Acknowledgments   6
Introduction, Sherrill Miller   7
A Male Perspective, Courtney Milne   9

CREATION, THE EARTH MOTHER   12
Neiterogob • Hera • Goddess of Laussel • Muk Juk • Spider Woman • Isis • White Buffalo Calf Woman • Neolithic Earth Mother • Cailleach Bheur • Copper Woman • Chaabou • Kunapippi • Lumimu'ut • Mu Olokukurtlisop • Lioramanpuel and Lijaramanpuel • Muzzu-Kummik-Quae

FERTILITY, THE FRUIT BEARER   34
Venus of Quinipily • Haumia and Rea • Freya • Astarte • Kutungga • Haumea • Sabra • Asintmah • Yaya-Zakura • Demeter • Estsan Atlehi • Yolkai Estsan • Paputuanuki

PURIFICATION, THE WATER GODDESS   50
Ganga • Machin Tungku • Hi'iaka • Chalchihuitlicue • The Norns • Sequana • Vulture Wife and Underwater Woman • Our Mother • Nyi Roro Kidul

TRANSFORMATION, THE WILD PSYCHE   62
The Black Madonna • Lilith • Kali • Oya • Inanna • Yeshe Khadoma • Kura Ngaituka • Pele • Birra-nulu • Old Woman • Hekate • Dzonokwa • Artemis-Diana • The Elbows Sharpened Women • Menily

INTEGRATION, THE HEALING SPIRIT   82
Mary • Asherah • Hathor • Gum Lin • Ixchel • Gyhldeptis • The Suleviae • Sophia • Sedna • Cha-dog-ma • Iduna

REVERENCE, THE MOUNTAIN DWELLER   96
Xi Wang Mu • Fuchi • Dewi Danu and Dewi Batur • Gokarmo • Parvati • Mama Paccha • Moombi • Gaia • Niangniang • Uma

ILLUMINATION, THE SKY DANCER   108
Tara • Ishtar • Kanene ski Amai yehi • Neith and Nut • !Urisis • Ol-apa • Wuriupranala • Yeshe Tsogyel • Pana • Aditi • Gauri • Amaterasu • Iris • Tree of Life

Bibliography   126

Acknowledgments

A big thanks to our friends and family who supported us through the preparation of this book.

Thank you to Laurie Ann Rayner for the computer imaging on several photographs, Richard Istace and Kevin Howell at YCC Digital Imaging for your technical assistance and care in digital scanning, and Gibson Photo in Saskatoon for your care and diligence in the E-6 processing of more than five thousand rolls of film over the past decade.

Our great appreciation to Patricia Langer, Rachel Pollack, Margaret Ponting, Leila Castle, Carole Nervig, Lexi Fisher and Kip Moore, Bettine Clemen, Haleh Samimi and Bruce van Goozen, Sara Comerford, Jackie Falardeau, Ruth Kinzel, Lyn Broughton-Kain and Sug Kain, Margo Anand, Thomas Moore and Dwayne E. Rourke for your personal communications and contributions to the manuscript. Thank you to Carolyn and William Chernenkoff for the countless Friday-night discussions on relationships and sexuality.

Thanks to our editors, Jackie Kaiser and Meg Taylor, designer Linda Gustafson and project coordinator Janice Brett, and to all the staff at Penguin Canada, for making our vision real.

A special acknowledgment to Ann Mortifee for sharing with us your pain, your joy and the authenticity of your struggle to honour the goddess within you.

To each of you, and to all who seek a union of the feminine and masculine within, we dedicate this book.

INTRODUCTION

Sherrill Miller

Our primary goal in *Visions of the Goddess* is to present the Earth Mother not just as a symbol, but as she was seen throughout antiquity – a vital energy manifested in the landscape. There was no separation between creation and the creative source, and this link between spirit and nature brought harmony and balance. In the West we have lost this union, and as a result we often feel detached from the world around us, left with a sense of anomie, or loss of spirit. This separation leads to a consolidation of control in the hands of the élite, to competition and inappropriate use of power, and to wars between people and nations. It can also be seen in the degradation of our environment and the astounding rate of species loss around the world.

While many books focus on the goddesses of classical and Old Europe, this book is designed to show the feminine in a global perspective. In our travels and readings, we found that almost every culture has at least one story of a goddess portrayed in the life-giving and death-wielding power of nature. With hundreds of goddesses to learn about, we felt a powerful affirmation that the sacred feminine is present everywhere, although subtly hidden in the mythologies of some cultures. Many pagan and animistic traditions acknowledge the primeval power of the goddess on a daily, seasonal and cyclical basis. Some places of worship embody her danger in volcanoes, her fecundity in the harvest or her renewability in sacred waters. Others symbolize her link to the unseen divine on mountains or express her spontaneity in the movements of the cosmos. These portrayals of natural earth temples and shrines within the landscape reinforce the connection between the sacred and the profane.

Feminist movements have clearly benefited from the rediscovery of the feminine spiritual voice. But the awakening of interest in historical goddesses has a much broader cultural significance, especially in the Western world. It is not just the feminine as embodied in women that benefits from this knowledge, but the feminine in all of us. The energy that is usually portrayed in qualities of gentleness, emotional expression, loving, caring and nurturing is as important to men as it is to women. It is the sprightly virgin energy that explodes with the joy of being young and curious. It is the spirit of the mother who protects, nurtures and sustains us. It is the wild woman who enlivens us, forcing us to experience the earthy depths of our darkest feelings, our physical urges and our mortality. It is the fierce energy and wisdom of the crone who brings us to our authentic power. In Western culture there is no feminine dimension in the collective image of the divine, no sacred entity that typifies a powerful feminine archetype capable of providing identity and sustenance to both women and men.

On August 31, 1997, the extent of this unmet need could be felt in the global response to the death of

Diana, Princess of Wales, and a week later to the death of Mother Teresa. According to Toronto healer Patricia Langer, the grief that surfaced – especially in the loss of Diana – expressed how much we as a culture had projected onto her the role of the feminine. She portrayed the innocent virgin, the fairy princess, the loving mother, the wounded wife, the out-of-control female and the transformed woman who was finally able to access her heart. We are now called upon to reclaim that projection, by acknowledging our power, by allowing transparency in our needs and feelings, and by acting on our capacity for unconditional love.

Our journey in quest of the Goddess has taken us to many unexpected places. One sojourn led to a small farmhouse in the back country of southwestern Saskatchewan. There, a man named Ted Douglas told us to "walk on uneven ground every day." This practice of walking on the earth, reminiscent of the Navajo ritual of Walking in Beauty, takes us back to the beginning of civilization, when humans first walked in the upright position. This integrates our spine, muscles and body organs, and keeps us in physiological balance. Perhaps this is the most ancient body memory we have, and is a way of bonding with the most primitive part of ourselves. If we believe in the collective unconscious, then our goal is to link ourselves to the experience and wisdom of all of our ancestors. We need to "remember" this experience – to reconnect it in our bodies, in our minds and in our hearts. It is a true reminder to be present in everything we do.

The origin of the word *saunter* comes to mind here. It is derived from the French *saint terre*, meaning "holy land." All indigenous cultures share a belief that the earth is "alive," especially at sacred sites where the Earth Mother or other gods and goddesses manifest themselves. This immanency of the divine in the landscape gives us a feeling of spiritual connection to the world around us.

The earth vibrates at a frequency of 8 hertz. When we walk in natural areas, our bodies resonate with and absorb this vibrational energy, which provides a feeling of harmony and relaxation. The asphalt of cities prevents us from walking directly on the land, and blocks the healing power of the earth. As a result, our bodies are subjected to tension that manifests itself in physical and emotional stress. It is no surprise that we often feel rejuvenated after walking by the sea, meandering in the forest or climbing a mountain.

The images in this book are meant to reconnect us to the vital world around us, and particularly to the feminine energy that sustains and nourishes. Each chapter is designed to portray the goddess energy that can transform one aspect of a symbolic life journey. Naming the goddesses and telling their stories brings them to life, allowing us to integrate their meaning into our lives. It is our hope that you will invite these images and stories to inspire you and that you will rejoice in the feeling of wholeness that comes from a reunion with our Earth Mother. May we all learn to walk again on uneven ground.

A MALE PERSPECTIVE

Courtney Milne

My first memories of the Earth Mother take me back to the age of four, when I lived overlooking a river and a park in the centre of town. It seemed to me that there was a great deal of magic out there in the trees and especially beside the fast-flowing water. My little heart yearned to know where the river went and where it came from, the parts hidden from view further intensifying the mystery. When I was old enough to manage a tricycle on my own, I pushed the pedals beyond my known world, along the park paths and around the corner to new territory, places that held promise of beauty and grandeur and terrible excitement – terrible because there were no answers, only more unsolved mysteries and more unexplored places, each time luring me further away from home.

Yet my early days in natural places also held for me a deep and abiding sense of security and reassurance. The river bank was a place that offered protection, security, even nurturance. When the "bad boys" from the fringe areas of town appeared on their bigger and faster bicycles, I could take refuge in the bosom of the Mother Goddess. I would hide in the bushes or in the cattails along the shore until they were safely out of sight. Her arms reached out to help me, and I knew

every tree and limb that was climbable to assure a swift escape. The more I became familiar with the natural surroundings, the more I felt that nature was like a friend I could trust and rely on to be there when needed.

In the summer I would pick the petunias in the flower-beds and make bouquets to celebrate the sheer joy of being out of school. We didn't call our two-month break a vacation; it was called summer holidays, and holidays were a time of thanksgiving and celebration. Then one day when I was seven, frivolity turned to dismay when my mother informed me that the petunias were not for picking but must remain in the park for all to enjoy. Once I learned the value of sharing, I became a staunch defender of the public flower-beds and became proud of the knowledge that I lived such a short distance to such unfathomable beauty.

Through the years the river maintained its hold on me, and when I finally had the means to make my own consumer decisions, a canoe was high on my list of priorities. The canoe in turn afforded me with opportunities for further wilderness exploration and a deepening awareness that I was much safer in the wilds than in places densely populated by human beings. Until the eleventh grade, when I grew 12 inches, I was shorter than the shortest girls in my class, which meant not only that I was bullied but also that I developed a kinship with the girls.

One advantage of having a female as a playmate is that you learn to use your imagination. I have one sister, and until adolescence disturbed the alchemy of familial bonds, we spent years playing together. Times with my sister and her friends involved a land of make-believe, trying out adult roles, exploring relationships and learning to get along. By contrast, my experiences with boys mostly involved sports – kicking, running, jumping and competing. Looking back, I value both sets of experiences, but I am particularly thankful for the sensitivities that I developed by nurturing my "feminine" side.

All of us – men, women, little girls and young boys, big or small – need the Goddess in our lives. She teaches us about the mysteries of nature and shows us how to live in harmony. She comes to us in many forms and resides within us in many ways. She teaches us to appreciate beauty, to identify, own and understand our feelings, to deal with our rage, to revel in our joys and to celebrate our sexuality. She shows us that we can ask for love, nourishment, friendship, softness, power, peace, laughter and wisdom. The Goddess never asks men – or women for that matter – to deny their masculinity. Instead she teaches us to own our entire range of feelings and emotions, encouraging us to delve into our shadows, and in so doing, get to know ourselves inside out. In the process, we become not only more content individuals but also better friends, lovers, parents, partners, merchants and leaders.

I feel both proud and privileged to be a landscape photographer, an outdoorsman and a student of goddess energies. In most of my photography I have attempted to interpret my joy in nature through straight, unmanipulated documentation of the world in front of the lens. In several instances I have recorded my "impression," using camera movement or multiple exposures. I have also enjoyed enhancing a number of images with the computer to better express a particular goddess or to create an image not possible with the camera alone. All special effects have been noted in the captions.

My experiences travelling the world have brought me delight, riches, warm friendships and hopefully some wisdom. My journeys in quest of Mother Nature's sacred places have even landed me with a goddess of my own, as en route I met my mate, Sherrill, the author of this book. Perhaps it was the fire goddess Fuchi who stirred me to attempt a marriage proposal in Japan, and maybe Spider Woman held us securely in her web of unity as we exchanged our wedding vows on a warm August afternoon in the park where I pedalled my tricycle when I was four. Returning to places of nourishment and honouring the special places of our childhood are important ways to rekindle the feelings of connectedness that so easily vanish when the web is torn.

Producing this book has taken Sherrill and me down an incredible pathway of adventure and experiences. Together we have ventured into the darkness of the cave, and we have bathed naked in radiant light. Happily the journey of discovery is not yet complete, and we offer you this book as a milestone, a place perhaps where our paths can cross, as all of us continue to seek our truths.

VISIONS OF THE GODDESS

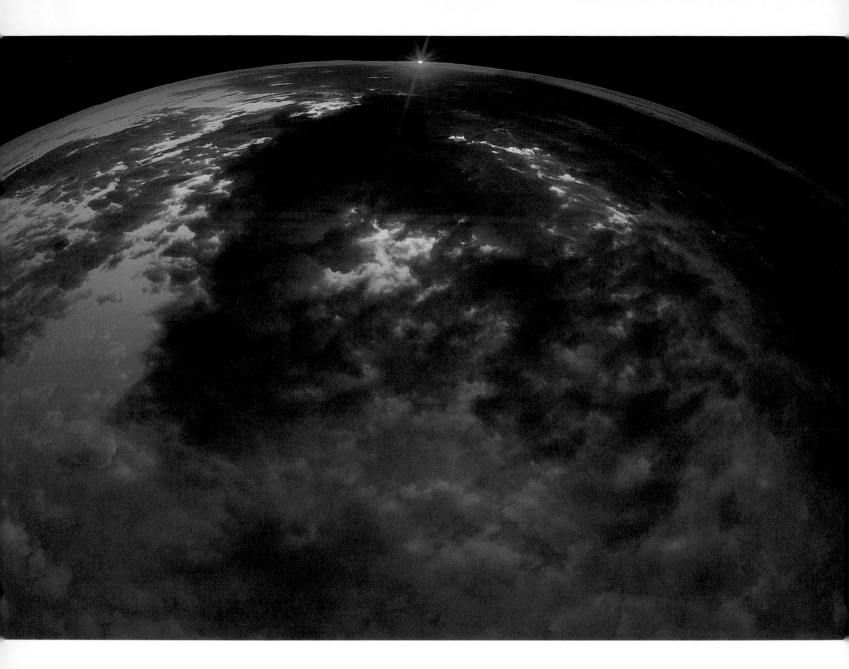

"Earth from Space." Sunset through fish-eye lens, inverted, 1983.

CREATION

The Earth Mother

The Earth Mother is the Great Goddess of the ancients, the all-encompassing creator who births herself and all the universe. This single figure embodies all stages of life as a triple goddess. She is the blossoming, life-giving Virgin (the word originally meaning "a woman unto herself"); the nurturing, fruit-bearing Mother; and the wise but death-bringing Crone. In her most ancient form in prehistoric culture, the body of the Great Goddess is the earth itself. Her womb is a cave deep in the earth, accessed through a narrow labyrinthine pathway that culminates in a grotto. As early as 30,000 BC, cave sanctuaries were places of ritual that were colourfully adorned with vibrant paintings of animal and human forms portraying the essence of life.

In subsequent cultures, the mother goddess remains rooted in the land. She is often called "All That Is," the goddess of ten thousand names who is the Great Mystery and the symbol of unity, holding the secrets of birth, death and regeneration. She is the sun, which provides light, warmth and sustenance, and the moon and stars, which brighten the night and regulate the passage of time. She is the essence of the rhythm of nature and the nurturing power that sustains all creation in her web of wisdom, which is the cauldron of life. Worshipped as the land itself and all its manifestations, the Earth Mother is the organic wholeness of nature, from which all life arises.

NEITEROGOB

Earth Mother of the Masai

Neiterogob, Earth Mother of the Masai, provides a
fertile environment for her people, who live off the
land. This ancient tribe of East Africa has always been
nomadic. To this day the Masai roam the *mara* or plains
between Kenya and Tanzania, herding their cattle as
they follow the water buffalo, gazelles and eland on
annual migrations in search of greener pastures provided by the seasonal rains. They often supplement
their herds with cattle stolen from other tribes along
the way – an honourable activity for the Masai warrior.

The staple food of the Masai is cow's blood,
drained from the living beast and curdled with milk.
This is considered to be the gift of the Earth Mother,
who provides for all her creatures.

Morning sun on the Masai Mara, Kenya, 1994.
Neiterogob provides the Masai with the gift of a new day.

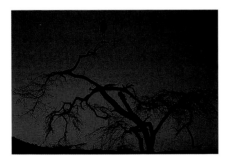

HERA

Mother Goddess of Greece

Mother goddesses in ancient Greece were known by
many names, depending on the cultural period.
The indigenous Pelasgians called her Eurynome,
referring to the wandering moon. Eurynome rose out
of Chaos and danced the world into being. In the later
Olympian version, Gaia is the first to emerge from
Chaos and create the earth. In classical Greece, it is
Hera, whose name means "mistress," a demotion of her
stature from its original power as the ancient Mother
Goddess. As consort of the sky god Zeus, Hera is given
a shrewlike role as the jealous wife of the powerful god
who frequently boasted of his liaisons with other
women.

In her Earth Goddess manifestation, Hera was
worshipped as ears of wheat, which were called the
"flowers of Hera" and placed as symbols of fertility and
abundance on her sacrificial altars. As Queen of the
Gods, she was often depicted seated on a majestic
throne between two lions, her crown of snakes reminiscent of the Neolithic Snake Goddess predominant
in the earlier Minoan culture of Crete.

*Wheat stocks, 1985. The "flowers of Hera" were
symbolic of her fertility as Mother Goddess.*

GODDESS
OF LAUSSEL

Paleolithic Mother

*Sculpture from rock face
at entrance to the cave
of Cap Blanc, near Les
Eyzies, France, 1995.*

Thirty thousand years ago, nomadic tribes made their homes in the fertile valleys of the Dordogne and Vézère rivers, leaving evidence of their habitation in cave paintings and female figurines, including the Goddess of Laussel. Although we cannot know for sure, the common speculation is that this goddess was a sacred image; her pregnancy, the feminine embodiment of the regenerative power of the universe. In her right hand she holds a notched bison horn, which is thought to symbolize the thirteen-month lunar calendar, while her left hand points to her vulva. The goddess figurines vary in shape and size, although the rounded buttocks, genital features and breasts are common. Some are incised with a variety of symbols from the natural world, including birds, wild animals or plants. Others are adorned with abstract symbols widely associated with the goddess, such as spirals, indicating the earth energy of the serpent and its transformative power, and meanders, wavy lines denoting the life-giving power of water. These decorations suggest an abiding connection between the symbol of the Earth Goddess and the elements of creation.

Mountainous natural stone formations still line the river valleys in what is now central France, their rock shelves and hollowed niches evidence of early habitation. By contrast, the painted caves of Paleolithic France and Spain (Lascaux, Pêche Merle, Les Trois Frères, Altamira and Chauvet, to name a few) were places of ritual rather than dwelling. In these labyrinthine passages deep in the earth, the bellylike cave of the Earth Goddess appears to be birthing the

La Montaigne rock formation, near Les Eyzies, France, 1995. Natural shelves and openings provided safe dwellings and shelter for nomadic people.

immense animal shapes, formed by the naturally contoured walls and highlighted by an ancient artist with streaks of red ochre, yellow and black pigments. Flickering light gives life to hunting scenes linked with shamanic images, perhaps depicting the mediation between the divine eternal world and the mundane. In other nearby caves, ancient stalagmites growing up from the earth echo another early goddess symbol: the pillar, or growing tree.

Apsara and strangler fig tree, Angkor Wat, Cambodia, 1992. The Earth Goddess, Muk Juk, asserts her power through nature as the tree roots destroy the sculpted deities on the cosmic mountain of stone.

MUK JUK

Black Lady of the Temple

The Earth Mother was called Black Lady by the indigenous people of Cambodia. Muk Juk's immense creativity is reflected in the overgrown strangler fig tree, its roots like a huge hand asserting her power in nature and dominating the monuments of humankind.

The temple city of Angkor Wat is an enormous complex built in the shape of a mountain, the archetypal symbol of a sacred place. Architects of the later Khmer dynasty designed this temple like a mandala, a magical representation of the mythical Mount Meru, the centre of the Hindu universe, where it is said that heaven meets earth. This is the home of the Brahman Sky God, Indra, who lives in a golden palace on the top of Mount Meru. The temple walls are sculpted with the ancient stories of the Vedic gods, and adorned with the Nymphs of the Lower Heavens, the celestial Apsaras or goddesses whose perfect beauty and alluring dance are meant only for the eyes of the gods. Today, in the name of the ancient Muk Juk, the jungle is reclaiming the land as well as the stone.

SPIDER WOMAN

Thinking Woman of the Pueblos

To the Pueblo cultures of the American southwest,
Spider Woman was known as Sussistannako or
Thinking Woman. The later Navajo people knew
her as the Earth Goddess, or Naestsan, the Woman
Horizontal, who created the winds that control all life
on earth and in the underworld. In her primordial
form, Spider Woman sat alone and spun a line in the
four directions and then sang her two daughters into
being. The daughters then created the sun and the
moon, and together with Spider Woman they made the
Star People, who were given clear crystal eyes so there
would never be complete darkness again.

Then Spider Woman created the people, using the
red, black, white and yellow clay colours of the earth.
To each she attached a thread of her web of wisdom,
which was connected to the doorway at the top of her
head, and she cautioned the people to always keep the
doorway open by chanting her songs. Many forgot or
were lost in floods and other disasters on the earth.
Finally, Spider Woman took those who remembered
into the Fourth World. She led them through the *sipapu*,
the opening for the spirits to enter the kiva, the sacred
ceremonial space that is the womb of Mother Earth. By
staying connected to her web, they would always be
able to draw on her wisdom in their travels.

*Composite of dew drops on spider web and Spider
Rock (computer enhanced), Canyon de Chelly, Arizona,
1990. Spider Woman's web allowed the people to stay
connected to her wisdom.*

ISIS

Mother Goddess of Egypt

Triple exposure of sun, moon and pyramids, Giza, Egypt, 1989. Isis is manifested in all aspects of the earth and the cosmos.

The cult of the goddess Isis existed prior to the dynasties of the Egyptian kings and extended from Egypt to the Middle East and as far north as Europe and Britain. Known as Lady of a Thousand Names, Isis is the eternal feminine, both in humankind and in nature. She is the universal goddess who rules all aspects of the earth, the seasons, the stars, the sun and the moon through her multiple manifestations.

Isis is unique in being the only Egyptian goddess with a personal story. Born of the sky goddess Nut and the earth god Geb, she is both sister and wife to the king, Osiris, and her power included ruling Egypt when he travelled. She taught spinning, weaving, grinding and the healing arts. When Osiris was killed by his brother Set, the tears of the grieving Isis caused the Nile to rise and flood the land, reflecting her queenly power to renew the earth and produce life-giving crops. Isis then manifested herself as the Neolithic Bird Goddess, fanning her great wings to bring Osiris back to life so he could impregnate her with their son Horus, the sun god. She subsequently used her magical embalming skills to revive Osiris, who became the ruler of the underworld.

The personification of Isis made her a mediator between the divine and the human realms, and may have been the Egyptian way of allowing humankind to relate to the unknowable face of divinity. The Egyptian goddess tradition persisted well into the second century, when the image of the goddess-mother and child-saviour was absorbed into the Christian symbol of the Virgin Mary and Christ child.

WHITE BUFFALO CALF WOMAN

Lakota Goddess of Harmony

Many creation stories of the native people of North America centre around vital life-giving female spirits. For the great Lakota (Oglala Sioux) nation of the Plains, it was White Buffalo Calf Woman (also known as Ta-tanka-wian-ska or Woope, and Ptesan Winyan to the Brulé Sioux) who came to their salvation. Clad in a dress of white buffalo hides decorated with porcupine quills, this beautiful maiden appeared to two young hunters looking for game to feed their starving people. Lusted after by the first hunter, she allowed him to embrace her, then reduced him to ashes in a cloud of white smoke. She then told the second man, who recognized her divinity and kept his distance, to return to the camp and prepare for her arrival. Entering the camp, she walked seven times around the central fire and gave the chief a ritual pipe with instructions on how to use it in seven ceremonies. She told them this was the third of seven revelations for the Oglala Sioux, and reminded them of the mysteries of their mother, the earth. Leaving her medicine bundle and promising to return one day, she then left the camp, transforming herself into a white buffalo.

Her legacy is relived in all Lakota religious rituals, which use pipes carved from a red stone quarry in southwestern Minnesota. Kinnikinnik, the sacred tobacco mixed with herbs, is lit with a buffalo chip, its smoke carrying the prayers of the people to Wakan Tanka, the Great Spirit. The bowl of the pipe represents the earth or the heart of the people, and holds the universe; the wood stem is all growing things; the incised buffalo portrays the connection between all land animals; and the twelve eagle feathers represent all winged creatures.

In the late 1800s, Black Elk, the great Lakota holy man, prophesied the return of White Buffalo Calf Woman in seven generations, when she would restore tranquillity to a troubled world. In August, 1994, in Janesville, Wisconsin, a white buffalo calf was born, reinforcing the belief in the return of White Buffalo Calf Woman to unify nations and bring harmony to the world.

Composite of pipestone quarry and bison (computer enhanced), Pipestone National Monument, Minnesota, 1993. White Buffalo Calf Woman vowed to return and bring harmony to the world.

NEOLITHIC EARTH MOTHER

Goddess of the Megaliths

Standing stones in dawn light, Avebury, England, 1989.
The megalithic monument is a legacy of the ancient goddess.

Following the retreat of the glaciers, the agrarian lifestyle was born, and with it a novel understanding of the earth. Humankind's new ability to co-create with nature was soon reflected in changing spiritual beliefs, as the ancient and all-encompassing Mother Goddess became differentiated into a number of deities who sanctified various aspects of life.

Goddess figures and ritual structures as old as 4000 BC have been found throughout mainland Europe, Malta and Britain, where thousands of megalithic tombs, stone circles, dolmens and passage graves were built to enable people to interact with the eternal earthly and celestial rhythms of the Goddess. The passage grave at Gavrinis, ornately carved with spirals and ancient patterns associated with the Earth Goddess, is oriented to the rising sun at the winter solstice. At nearby Carnac, three thousand standing stones stretch in lines for more than 4 kilometres (2 miles). In Britain, the original temple of Stonehenge, dated before 2800 BC, was aligned with the cycles of the moon, while subsequent builders in 2400 BC set stones in relation to the sun. The rings of standing stones at Avebury originally took the form of a giant serpent with two egglike shapes in its belly, although only parts of the outer circle remain. In the Outer Hebrides, off the windswept coast of Scotland, the Standing Stones of Callanish are aligned with a series of lunar movements reflected in the landscape. Despite this diversity of forms, the original sense of unity with a single mother goddess presiding over all creation is maintained.

Spiral patterns on stones of passage grave, Gavrinis, France, 1995. Spiral and meander patterns represent the ancient Goddess.

CAILLEACH BHEUR

Ancestress of Stones

Double exposure of Standing Stones of Callanish with moon, Callanish, Scotland, 1989. The Neolithic Moon Goddess is honoured in the stone circle.

This divine Celtic ancestress is the Hag of Winter, the wise old woman who created megalithic monuments when she dropped stones from her apron. The handiwork of the Cailleach Bheur can be see at the Clava Cairns in Scotland, where rings of standing stones encircle two burial mounds called passage graves. The openings to the mounds, which are aligned with the southwest setting sun on the summer solstice, lead to passages that terminate in large central chambers used for human burials. This mysterious place nestled in a grove of trees imbues the visitor with a sense of peace. (See back cover.)

Smoky peat fires permeate the mists swirling in the persistent dampness of the islands sacred to the Celtic Great Goddess, Brigid, who is also called Bride. The Outer Hebrides are home to many ancient monuments, including the Standing Stones of Callanish (Gaelic: Calanais). From a distance, the main circle looks like jagged toothpicks stuck by the Cailleach into the rolling hills, which in September when we visited were coated with copper-hued heather still tinged with the leftover bloom of summer purple. The central chambered mound of Callanish forms the circle of a flattened Celtic cross, with three small avenues of stones aligned with various star constellations. The main avenue of thirty-nine guardian stones, 90 metres (295 feet) in length, includes some stones more than 3 metres (10 feet) high. Many of these stones are imbedded with white crystal or hornblende, which is said to account for the high vibrational energy that some visitors feel here.

Across Loch Roag, the Earth Goddess can be seen as the Cailleach na Mointeach, the Sleeping Beauty, her contours in the Pairc Hills clearly outlined against the sky. The lunar standstill, a unique astronomical phenomenon that occurs every 18.5 years, can be viewed from the avenue stones at Callanish. The full moon moves over the body and face of the sleeping Goddess, then skims the east row of standing stones and disappears from view in a notch behind the hill called Cnoc an Tursa (Hill of Mourning). Moments later, the darkness is relieved when the moon miraculously returns to shine at the head of the burial cairn and beneath the foot of the largest stone at Callanish. Thus, it appears the ancient Celtic people perfectly mapped the symbolic birth of the moon from the Earth Mother.

Composite of sunset sky and Pairc Hills (computer enhanced), Callanish, Scotland, 1995.

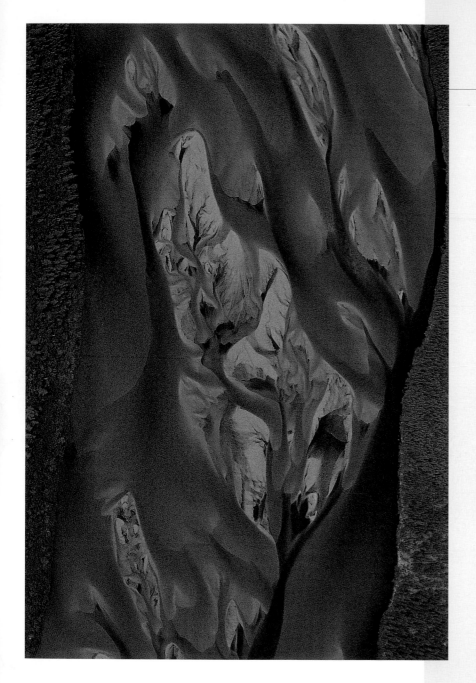

COPPER WOMAN

Primeval Woman of the Dene

The Athabascan tribes of northern Canada valued copper for its sheen and malleability for making knives and other tools. Many stories are told of the primeval goddess who was responsible for the highly prized mineral. As First Woman of the Dene people, Copper Woman had sex with a dog who became a man at night. Together they had six puppies, three of which became humans, the ancestors of the Athabascan tribes, known as the Dogrib or dog-sided people. The Chipewyan, a tribe of Dene people who settled around Lake Athabasca in northern Saskatchewan, tell the story of Copper Woman's being abducted and made pregnant by an Eskimo. She escaped, fleeing with her child over the great water, guided by a wolf who led her to the fiery yellow nuggets so valued by her people.

Aerial view of sand formations in William River, Lake Athabasca, Saskatchewan, 1993. Copper Woman, the Keeper of the Minerals and First Woman of the Dene and Chipewyan, moves through the landscape.

CHAABOU

Nabatean Earth Mother

The Arabian goddess Al Lat was worshipped at Mecca for more than one thousand years before the arrival of Islam in the seventh century. In the matriarchal culture of the Koreshites, Mohammed's tribespeople, Al Lat was honoured as a triple goddess: as Kore, the virgin crescent moon; as Al Uzza, the full moon of the fruitful mother; and as Al Menat, the waning crone or Old Woman of prophecy and divination. The initial laws of the Koran, the Word of Kore, are attributed to the seven priestesses of the goddess temple at Mecca. The deity there was Shayba (or Sheba), the Old Woman who was worshipped in the form of a black aniconic stone, a piece of meteorite apparently valued for its celestial origins. It is inscribed with the yoni, the ancient shape that is universally symbolic of the female vulva and of feminine regenerative power.

When Mohammed returned from being cast out of Mecca, he introduced the new religion of Islam, but left the goddess symbols in place, eventually enshrining the Black Stone on the corner of the Kaaba, the large block of stone dedicated to Allah. During the ritual haji required of all Muslims, pilgrims kiss the stone of the Goddess, which is still guarded by the priests of the Kaaba, who are called Beni Shaybah, the Sons of the Old Woman.

Detail of sandstone wall, Petra, Jordan, 1990. The body of Chaabou, the Earth Mother, is portrayed in the patterns of nature.

The ancient Arabian Mother Goddess, Shayba, reappears as Chaabou, mother of Dusares, the revered god of a tribe called the Nabateans. Chaabou was glorified in her temple at Petra, the sandstone city of antiquity built at the crossroads of the Silk Road trade routes in the desert of present-day Jordan. In this monumental city carved from the living rock, Chaabou was renowned. Her cult has been compared to that of the goddess Demeter in Hellenic Greece.

KUNAPIPPI

Mother of All

Kunapippi, the Aboriginal mother of all living things, came from a land across the sea to establish her clan in northern Australia, where she is found in both fresh and salt water. In the Northern Territory she is known as Warramurrungundji. She may also manifest herself as Julunggul, the rainbow snake goddess of initiations who threatens to swallow children and then regurgitate them, thereby reinforcing the cycle of death and rebirth. In Arnhem Land she is Ngaljod, the rainbow snake who causes water holes to overflow and drown people who do not look after the land according to the laws of the Dreamtime. Ngaljod also works with Nammarkan, the lightning man, who strikes thunder off the clouds and brings the rainy season to renew the land.

During female puberty rites an initiate goes into seclusion to avoid attracting Ngaljod's attention, after which the girl is covered with red ochre, a white crescent moon is painted below her breasts to help regulate her menses, and sometimes a depiction of Ngaljod is painted between her breasts.

Pictograph, Kakadu National Park, northern Australia, 1989. The wife of Nammarkan, the lightning man, with spirit figures (1964 painting by Najombolmi, the last great traditional artist of the Gagadju people). (below) Kunapippi is found in both fresh and salt water.

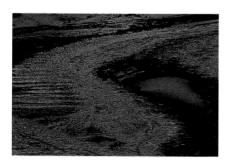

LUMIMU'UT

Mother of the Gods

Myths of the archipelagos of Southeast Asia tell
of primal female deities originating from stones.
Lumimu'ut, the Earth Goddess of several island cultures of Indonesia, was born from the sweat of a rock.
A crane then directed her to find soil to cover the rock
and make the earth, including all the mountains and
rivers. After this was done, she planted the seeds of
trees and all the plants to grow on the earth. Later, she
climbed to the top of one of her mountains, where she
was impregnated by the West Wind and bore the gods
and all the humans to populate the land.

In Bali today, religious festivals frequently revolve
around a sacred tree that is said to be the link between
heaven and earth. It is decorated with colourful cloths
that are a feminine symbol in memory of the Goddess.

East coast of Bali and Sea of Java, Indonesia, 1989.
Lumimu'ut, Mother Goddess of Indonesia, was
born from the sweat of a rock.

Underwater sea life, Gulf of Panama, 1995. Nets of gold and silver caught the food spilling from Golden Salt Tree Woman.

MU OLOKUKURTLISOP

Luminescent Giant Butterfly Lady

Mu is the Mother of the Cuna people, who live in the jungles of eastern Panama and on the San Blas islands off the coast. The dead rest with her spirit in a womb cave situated on the Gulf of Darien. In a nearby women's shrine, young girls reaching puberty are honoured with a secret Cuna name. In this sacred grove, the initiate is painted with the red fruit of the saptur trees, said to contain the juice of the menstrual blood of Mu.

As a giver of life, Mu Olokukurtlisop was also manifested as the Golden Salt Tree Woman, whose top branches held fish, animals, birds and vegetables. The sun shaman Ibele desired to retrieve this bounty by cutting the tree. The hard trunk resisted, and any damage was repaired by jaguars, who licked the cut to heal it. When Ibele's brother killed these animals and the tree was finally toppled, water poured out to form the ocean, and abundant food was caught in nets of gold and silver spread below.

LIORAMANPUEL
and
LIJARAMANPUEL

Earth Women of Pohnpei

The ancient god of the islands of Micronesia knew
that land would be found where the sky roof touched
the sea, so Sapkini prepared a strong canoe and sent
his people to find it. Many women helped with the
voyage, including Lisapikini, Woman of Little Rain,
and Lieulele, Woman of Clear Weather. Birds guided
them to a distant coral reef, where the Stabilizer of the
Shore was called to secure the coastline and be sure
the mangrove trees took root. Then the two Earth
Women, Lioramanpuel and Lijaramanpuel, dug earth
from the sea and made a platform, which they called
pei, meaning stone altar. Then they piled it high with
earth and called it *pohn*; thus the name of the island
was Pohnpei, meaning "upon a stone altar." All the people returned home except Limeutu, the creator goddess who stayed with her husband to guard the new
land and bore many children to populate the island.
When Limeutu became old, she did not die but transformed into a small flying creature who still inhabits
the island.

*Vegetation on Pohnpei, seen through fish-eye lens,
Micronesia, 1989. Lioramanpuel and Lijaramanpuel
made a platform piled high with earth to create the
island of Pohnpei.*

MUZZU-KUMMIK-QUAE

Earth Woman of the Anishinabe

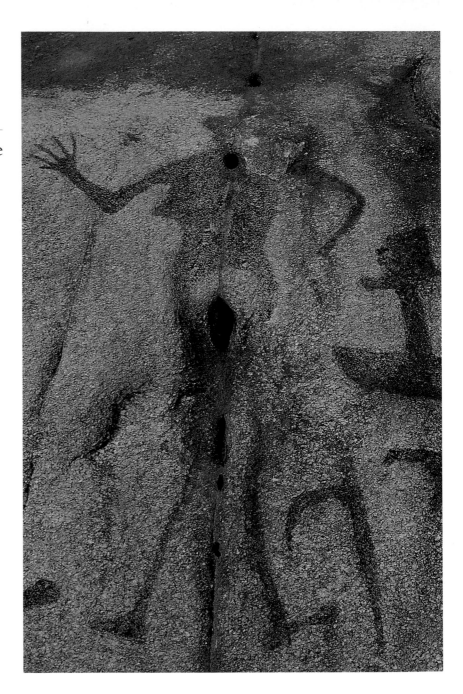

Pictograph at "Teaching Rocks," Petroglyphs Park, Ontario, 1985. The fissure in the rock is said to be an entrance to the underworld or the symbolic womb of the Earth Mother.

For the Anishinabe, the Original People of the Odawa, Potawatomi and Ojibway nations of North America, Muzzu-Kummik-Quae, or Earth Woman, is the mother of all creation. Not only does she provide for all her people's physical needs, but her beauty and abundance continually inspire them with the mystery of life. Earth Woman's fertility and her changing seasons are a reflection of the power of the Great Spirit, Gitchi Manitou, the creator of all things, who infused all the plants and animals with the spirit of life. The Anishinabe offer thanks to the Great Spirit for the seven sacred teachings given to Original Man in the shape of petroforms, a gift to the Earth Mother at Manito Ahbee.

The power of Muzzu-Kummik-Quae is illustrated in the story of Nanabush, the trickster and spiritual guide of the Anishinabe. One day he was camped by a stream when suddenly the waters began to rise. He could not escape the inundation even though he retreated to the highest mountain. There he was able to salvage two logs and make a raft, but even the manitous (spirits) could not help him or the dying creatures around him. Suddenly he remembered how Geezhigo-Quae, or Sky Woman, had restored the earth during another flood, but he knew he did not have the power of a manitou. In his desperation, he asked the animals to help him, and the muskrat dove deep into the water and brought him a pawful of soil. Like Sky Woman, he blew into the soil, and it began to grow until an island was formed. Nanabush realized he could not have done this alone. His life had depended on the logs and creatures of the Earth Mother.

Composite of moon, forest and petroform (computer enhanced), Whiteshell Provincial Park, Manitoba, 1993. Muzzu-Kummik-Quae is the mother of all creation.

Tropical vegetation, Hawaii, 1987. Haumea's domain is the forest.

FERTILITY

The Fruit Bearer

The original feminine deity, the Great Mother, is the all-encompassing goddess of ancient cultures who controlled every aspect of life and death. After the retreat of the glaciers and the establishment of the first Neolithic settlements, the single image of the Earth Mother started to evolve into a variety of goddesses with more specific manifestations and roles. The Lady of Plants and Animals, the Bird Goddess and other nature deities gradually emerged from a pastoral lifestyle and understanding of agriculture. Domestication of animals provided a new concept – the mystery of birth – and displayed both life and death as part of the cycle.

In the fullness of her womanhood as the ripeness of summer, the Fruit Bearer is seen to control the rhythm of life and the seasons of cultivation. The cyclical nature of life is ensured through annual rituals associated with cultivating the land, planting the seeds, nourishing the first growth, harvesting the crop and tending newborn animals. The fertility goddess presides over both female and male puberty rites to guide the initiates to their full creative potential and the perpetuation of the tribal line. She evokes feelings of sexual desire and offers the pleasures of physical lovemaking. The Fruit Bearer is now invoked in all her aspects of sexual flowering, as she manifests herself in prolific fertility, birthing rituals, vibrant sexuality and abundant vegetation.

VENUS OF QUINIPILY

Spirit of Isis

Double exposure of Venus of Quinipily and rock wall in garden near Baud, France, 1995. (below) Standing stone, Carnac, France, 1995.

The province of Brittany, in France, is littered with megalithic monuments dating to the Neolithic period. It is dominated by the menhirs ("long stones") of Carnac, the rows of standing stones erected as monuments to the Earth Mother worshipped here for thousands of years. This goddess tradition was continued by the later Celtic and Roman tribes, and local lore speaks of a Roman goddess known as the Venus, or the Egyptian deity Isis, who was beseeched to help ease the pains of childbirth. Her statue was mysteriously stolen and thrown into the river many times throughout the seventeenth century. Because the largest nearby town of Auray is a Christian pilgrimage centre dedicated to Saint Anne, it is thought the culprits were Christians who objected to the worship of pagan idols. After each incident, the Venus was salvaged by locals and re-erected, until a native benefactor, the Count of Lannion, finally rescued the statue and placed it in the Chateau de Quinipily, his garden estate near Baud. There the Venus of Quinipily is now protected and lovingly tended by aged caretakers who live on the site.

HAUMIA and REA

Maori Goddesses of the Forest

In the folklore of the Maori people of New Zealand, the forest is a place of the spirits and a storehouse of food. The goddess Rea, meaning "sheen," is said to be embodied in the light green hues of the large plants. Her role is to protect the nature spirits below her on the forest floor.

Haumia-tikitiki, one of the seventy children of the ancestral parents Rangi and Paputuanuki (Papa), is the goddess of the *aruhe*, the edible fern root that provides an important source of food. *Aruhe* is also worn as an amulet to protect people from the curse of witches and from a variety of illnesses. Being a root, Haumia is sheltered in the body of the Earth Mother, and Papa's body must be entered carefully. Special chants are sung to ensure a good harvest of *aruhe*, and it is said that sometimes Haumia can be heard speaking as the root diggers work the earth.

Ferns, New Zealand, 1984. Haumia and Rea protect the nature spirits, as well as people.

FREYA

Nordic Queen of the Gods

Detail of volcanic cindercone, Iceland, 1993.
Freya displayed her magic throughout the land.

Like deities in other cultures, the Nordic goddesses appear in many forms as spirits who preceded the patriarchal gods of the Aesir. Freya probably was derived from the early Germanic goddess Frea, who could fly like a bird. As supreme mistress and guardian of fertility and sexuality, Freya took all the gods as lovers, and as the ruler of death, she led the war maiden Valkyries. In her matronly form as Frigg, she is Queen of Heaven, later designated as the wife of the god Odin. In her form as the goddess Thorgerd, she wept tears of gold as she rode her golden boar through the forest; as Gefion (or "giving"), her role is the ancient woman giant who ploughed the earth into the sea, creating the land of Zealand, now known as Holland. Freya's magic was powerful, and her cult lasted long past the advent of Christianity and is still acknowledged through her sacred day, Friday, which is thought to be the luckiest day for a wedding.

Icelandic sagas recorded in the Elder Edda (tenth century) and the Prose Edda (fourteenth century) report tales of Freya's journeying through the land answering prophetic questions or flying on her cat-drawn chariot. She is identified by her famous amber necklace of blazing fire, the Brisingamen, known as the "rainbow bridge to paradise." Freya felt compelled to have the necklace, which had been mysteriously crafted by four dwarfs. They gave it to her after she agreed to spend a night with each of them. When she wore the magical necklace, the stones reflected the lights of the rainbow, the glow of dawn, the burning setting sun and the glistening morning star.

Volcanic rock, Iceland, 1993. Freya's necklace shone with all the colours of the rainbow.

Garden vegetation, Israel, 1989. Astarte manifests herself as the spirit of both death and life.

ASTARTE

Lady of Death and Life

Astarte, "she of the womb," is the spirit of sexuality and the goddess of desire. Myth says she descended to earth from Venus and landed at Byblos, near present-day Mount Carmel, Israel. She was worshipped here until the fourth century, when the Christian emperor Constantine closed all goddess shrines. In Canaan she is known as Anat, the great creator and destroyer who is wife and sister of the god Baal, whom she rescues from death in the underworld with the help of the sun goddess Shapash. Her untrammelled sexuality is equalled by her destructive nature, with her rage for blood so strong that legends say she slew all the celebrants in a victorious battle feast on the mountain of heaven.

Despite her wild sexual nature, Astarte did not bear children. For this she was denigrated by the Hebrews in the Old Testament, which refers to her as Ashtoreth, a distortion of her name such that it means "shameful thing."

KUTUNGGA

Aboriginal Spirit Mother

*Boulders of Uluru (Ayers Rock), Australia, 1989.
Kutungga's offspring gave birth to an endless
number of spirit children known as Yulanya.*

Kutungga, a prolific mother goddess of the Australian
Aboriginals, produced offspring who were transformed into egg-shaped boulders. The wise women of
this Aboriginal culture are honoured for their magical
powers and sacred knowledge. Tales of the Dreamtime
tell of men who stole the sacred bag of wisdom from
the women, but it is recognized that women retain the
greatest power of all in their wombs.

Detail at Hilo Gardens, Island of Hawaii, 1987.
Shreds of Haumea's clothing cling to the vines.

HAUMEA

Mother Goddess of Hawaii

This fertility goddess is called the Mother of Hawaii.
As the mother guardian and divine ancestress of
the Hawaiian people, her name means "the one from
whom the land is born." She gave birth not only to the
Hawaiian people, but also to two legendary daughters,
the fiery volcano goddess Pele, and Hi'iaka, the patron
goddess of the sacred hula dance. Although Haumea
has a destructive aspect (she sent Pele to destroy everything in her path), she is also the creation deity who
taught Hawaiian women how to birth their children
by pushing them out of the womb. Before she taught
them this, babies were cut out through the abdomen.

As a goddess of love and sexuality, Haumea has
magical powers of rejuvenation. She never grows
old but continuously transforms herself into a young
woman to mate with a multitude of men. When one
of her favourite partners, Wakea, was about to be sacrificed, she took him into her forest domain, carrying
him to safety by running directly through the tree
trunks, leaving shreds of her colourful clothing hanging on the vines. As a goddess of wild plants, Haumea
can make the sacred fruit trees produce at her com-
mand, and she can use her magic staff to fill the waters
with fish. But if angered, Haumea may withdraw her
energy and leave her people to starve.

SABRA

The Rescued Princess

According to a Syrian legend, Sabra, the mythical virgin daughter of an Egyptian king, was chained to a rock as a sacrifice to a dragon. The dragon (or serpent) was in many cultures a manifestation of the ancient chthonic goddess who lives deep in the earth. In the name of Christianity, Saint George slayed the dragon and rescued Sabra from this pagan ritual. A shrine dedicated to this saint is located in northern Syria, where barren women continue to go to seek fertility.

Saint George represents the earthly aspect of the Archangel Michael, who was said to appear in visions during the fifth century. He is immortalized at Mont St.-Michel, the fairy-tale abbey on a rocky island that is 80 metres (250 feet) high and sits off the coast of Normandy. According to the Apocalypse book of Saint John the Apostle, Michael, the Prince of the Heavenly Host, slew the seven-headed dragon that threatened the Virgin Mary and her Holy Child.

In pagan times the mountain was called Dinsul, the Holy Mount of the Sun, known in Celtic mythology as one of the sea tombs harbouring souls of the dead. The original tenth-century church, Notre-Dame-sous-la-Terre (Our Lady Underground), was built when the abbey was founded and is now a crypt with the nave of the Romanesque church constructed over it.

The main cathedral spire, rising 152 metres (499 feet) above the sea, is crowned with a golden statue, 5 metres (15 feet) high, of Saint Michael displaying his prowess, his sword drawn as he kills the dragon.

Depending on the lunar and solar orbits, the tides here can vary by 15 metres (49 feet), a testament to the power of natural forces, which were so honoured in the Celtic world. This prominent Catholic pilgrimage site is completely surrounded by the sea at high tide, reinforcing the association with the ancient goddess and Mary, the Christian mother image, who is often called "the sea."

Mont St.-Michel and setting sun, Normandy, France, 1995. The cathedral of Saint Michael immortalizes the slayer of the dragon, symbol of the pagan goddess.

Multiple exposure of fireweed and log house, Yukon Territory, 1988. Asintmah wove a sacred blanket of fireweed, Earth's favourite herb.

ASINTMAH

Weaver of Fireweed

The First Woman of the Tlinget people, Asintmah initially appeared near the Athabasca River in northern Saskatchewan, Canada. As Earth Mother, she walked over the land, collecting fallen branches to make her loom. Asintmah wove a blanket from the fibres of fireweed, the willow herb loved by Earth. Then she gathered the sacred cover and walked in all four directions, spreading it over Earth's body and anchoring each corner to the sacred peaks of Sharktooth Mountain, Pillar of Rock, Levelhead Mountain and Mount Atiksa. Finally, Asintmah wove threads of music and sang as Earth heaved and birthed her children, bringing Mouse, Rabbit, Cougar, Caribou and all the other animals onto the land.

YAYA-ZAKURA

Goddess of Spring

In Shinto belief, nature reveals the sacred. Every aspect of nature contains resident *kami* – spirits that inspire awe. This spiritual ambience in nature brings one into the presence of the transcendent aspects of existence as long as one practises purity and devotion, not only by pilgrimage to specific shrines, but by honouring the sun and the emperor. The name *Japan* comes from the kanji characters meaning "root of the sun," which explains the choice of the sun as the national symbol and the worship of the Imperial household as the sun's embodiment.

Cherry blossom time in Japan is a national celebration of a sacred season, when every part of the country follows the progression of flowering as it starts in the south and advances to the north throughout the month of April. Newspapers relay this information for travellers wishing to journey to the best viewing places, and railway stations display the Sakura Viewing Timetable, labelled with flowers in various stages of bloom.

Yaya-Zakura, the Shinto goddess of the cherry tree, can often be seen as a white cloud over Fujisan, the sacred Shinto mountain. She is said to remain celibate during the beauty of her blossoming each spring. However, when her petals fall to the ground, Yaya-Zakura is able to take lovers and enjoy the fruitfulness of her sacred season.

Sakura blossoms, Nara, Japan, 1988. Yaya-Zakura takes lovers only after her blossoms have fallen to the ground.

DEMETER

Great Goddess of
Olympian Greece

Stream and dying vegetation, Greece, 1989. When Kore was abducted to the underworld, Demeter's grief caused darkness to fall over the land.

As Mother of the Soil and of the Grain, Demeter controls the fertility of the land. She is immortalized in the classical Greek mythology of the Eleusinian Mysteries, the annual sacred rites that re-enacted the abduction of her daughter, Kore. As Kore was picking a narcissus in the gardens of Eleusis, she disappeared through a crevice in the earth and was abducted to the underworld to become the wife of Hades. For nine days Demeter searched for her daughter, her grief causing the flowers and crops of the Rharian Plain to dry and wither. Finally Hecate, the crone, met Demeter by the spring of Eleusis and told her of Hades' plan to marry Kore, a plan that had been sanctioned by Zeus. Demeter bargained with Zeus to have Kore returned. But Kore had eaten six seeds of the pomegranate, the fruit of knowledge of the underworld and the symbol of fertility that brings about rebirth. Zeus therefore decreed that Kore must live for half the year as Persephone, Queen of the Underworld.

Throughout antiquity, the Greater Mysteries of Demeter were re-enacted in the autumn, the time of the sowing of seeds. The vision-seeking initiates, the *mystai*, first bathed in the sea at Phaleron, then held rituals that culminated in the processional walk along the ancient Sacred Way from Athens to Eleusis, the Place of Happy Arrival. Passing Demeter's holy fig tree, they entered the sacred precinct and gathered at a darkened cave, the symbolic entrance to the underworld. As they sang and chanted, torchlight suddenly blazed forth out of the blackness, signalling the return of Kore and the renewal of the fertility of the land.

ESTSAN ATLEHI

Mother of All

As Navajo Mother of All Life, Estsan Atlehi birthed the earth and all the processes of nature. Estsan Atlehi epitomizes the changes seen in the rhythm of the seasons, the phases of the moon and the life cycle of all her people on earth. She teaches her people to walk the Trail of Beauty and to keep her ways alive by chanting the ritual songs of the Blessing Way. In her manifestation as Changing Woman or Asdzaa Nadleehe, she guides the Kinaalda, the coming-of-age ritual for girls entering puberty, by demonstrating how she can rejuvenate herself through the cycle of life from virgin, to woman, to wisdom keeper.

Antelope Canyon, Page, Arizona, 1993. As Mother of All, Estsan Atlehi portrays the rhythm of life in canyons the Navajo call Tse'neh'eh'diz'sjaa, "Where water paints a picture of itself."

Sunlight through silica crystal, 1990. White Shell Woman formed a circle of turquoise and white shells, then created a burst of light in a rock of crystal.

YOLKAI ESTSAN

Bringer of Light

In her manifestation as White Shell Woman, or Yolkai Estsan, Navajo Changing Woman is a moon goddess made from abalone shell, a symbol of her colourful beginnings. To the Apache, she is White Painted Woman, who was warned by the Giver of Life of a coming deluge. He directed her to take refuge in an abalone shell, which carried her to White Sands, in present-day New Mexico, where she gave birth to two children, Son of the Sun and Child of the Water.

As the ruler of the east, Yolkai Estsan was born in a cradle of rainbows with the first glow of dawn at her feet. As the primordial creator, she made the first woman from yellow corn and the first man from white corn. To bring light to the dark and troubled world, she formed a circle of turquoise and white shells. Then she held a rock of crystal and used all of her powers to bring forth a burst of light, creating the gift of fire for her people on earth.

PAPUTUANUKI

Earth Mother of the Maori

Paputuanuki, the Maori Earth Mother, and her consort Rangitane, Father Sky, came from the mythical land of Hawaiiki, the paradise to the east. In the darkness they embraced until all living things grew between their bodies. Their children wanted out into the light but could not separate from them. Finally their eldest son, Tane Mahuta, the god of the forests, was able to push them apart with the help of chanting by Whaityri, the underworld goddess of thunder and lightning. When Earth Mother and Father Sky were finally separated, their offspring became all the elements of the cosmos and the earth, and the creation of the world was completed. However, the primordial parents still remain connected by her rising heat and his falling rain.

Clouds over New Zealand, 1984. The rising heat of the Earth Mother, Paputuanuki, maintains her connection with Father Sky.

Waterfall and pool, central Iceland, 1992. Urth's waters nourished the sacred World Tree,
Yggdrasil, which held the universe together.

PURIFICATION

The Water Goddess

Water is often seen as a purifier as well as a symbol of the emotional journey through life. The water goddess is embodied in this mythical flow of life, and through this medium she provides cleansing, nourishment and sensuous enjoyment. She can be unpredictable in her hidden depths or dangerous in her angry moods, when she is capable of swallowing everything in her path. She is portrayed in the immensity of the ocean of existence and in the delicacy of dewdrops nourishing the earth or coalescing to form the spring of life. Her manifestations seduce and cajole the spirit to constantly move, adjust and glide through life. Only in the rare stillness of a deep pool does she allow quiet reflection. Her cleansing power is not one of removing the dirt or grime of life, but of the purification that fosters transition and transformation.

The water goddess is mutable, versatile and full of energy and excitement, her fluidity allowing her to constantly create new forms. She can be seen embodied in the flexibility of the hula dance and in the abundance of life-giving rains. Her torrents may rage and carve a destructive path that becomes a vehicle for regeneration and rebirth. The gentle flow of her streams may provide redemption and eternal life while the moisture of her womb is manifested in the grace found in baptismal fonts and healing wells.

GANGA

Goddess of Purification

The divine Ganga, the wife of all the celestial gods, is manifested in the waters of the Ganges River. Daughter of the Mountain Mother, Nanda Devi, Ganga was invited from heaven to purify the ashes of sixty thousand sons of the sage Bhagirath so they could reach paradise. She flowed in immense torrents from the great toe of the god Shiva, and would have flooded the earth had Shiva not caught her waters in his matted hair; thus Shiva earned the designation Ganga-dhara, Upholder of the Ganges. Ganga's most sacred site is Benares (Varanasi), where she baptizes and redeems souls. Pilgrims flock here to bathe in and drink the sacred waters. Funeral pyres are located on the ghats, steps leading down to the Ganges; the ashes of the devout are then sprinkled on the flowing water, which gives everlasting release from sins, as garlands of yellow and orange flowers are offered in honour of Ganga.

The Ganges River, Benares, India, 1989. Pilgrims bathe in the waters of Ganga, receiving purification and release from their sins.

MACHIN TUNGKU

Mother of Water

As Mother Guardian of Water, this deity of the indigenous Mon people of Burma plays an important role
in an agrarian culture that is still dependent on its
waterways for both transportation and farming.
Machin Tungku shares importance with another
goddess, Chang-hko, the primeval mother who sur-
vived in a boat during the mytho-historical great flood
to become the mother of the Kachin people. These
female deities also appear in the form of *nats*, the elemental earth spirits who live throughout the universe
in water, on land and in the heavens. Every house has
its complement of *nats*, who must be indulged and
cared for "like a husband," to protect the family from
any harm. *Nats* are said to gather in haunted places,
especially the confluence of rivers, where village
ceremonies invoke Machin Tungku and the *nat* spirit,
Lady of the River, to protect the land and produce a
good rice crop.

*Sunset on the Irrawaddy River, Burma, 1991. Machin
Tungku shares her domain with the* nat *spirit, Lady of
the River.*

Haena Point, Na Pali coast, Kauai, Hawaii, 1987. Hi'iaka, the deity of the hula, can be seen at Kee Beach.

HI'IAKA

Patroness of the Hula

Hi'iaka, "the cloudy one," is one of many beautiful daughters of Hawaii's fertile mother goddess Haumea. From her armpit, Haumea created the volcanic fire goddess Pele. Then, from her mouth, Haumea produced Hi'iaka in an egg. Pele carried the egg under her armpit until her sister was born. Pele sent Hi'iaka, her favourite sister, to the island of Kauai to bring back Pele's lover, Chief Laka. When they were late getting back, the fiery Pele took vengeance by burning Hi'iaka's beloved forests and killing Hi'iaka's friend, the poet Hopoe. On their arrival, Pele killed Chief Laka, but Hi'iaka used her magical powers to restore him to life. The two then fled far from Pele's reach and returned to the Na Pali coast on the island of Kauai. They lived together here at Laka's court, where the sacred hula dance was performed. At the nearby Kailua Heiau temple, Hi'iaka supervised the initiation rites of the priestesses, who were required to dive from the cliff top into the waves below and then swim ashore to Kee Beach.

CHALCHIHUITLICUE

Mistress of the Rains

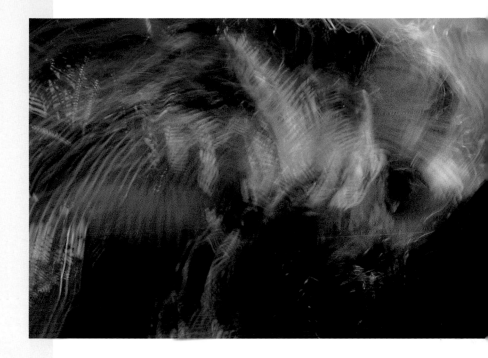

Camera movement on palm fronds, 1988. The Mistress of Rains and Waters ruled during a time of chaos.

In the Mayan sacred texts, called the Chilam Balam, many water goddesses are proclaimed, perhaps to control the rains sent from the creator Hunab, who periodically unleashed torrents of water from the belly of the sky serpent. These people of the lowlands of Mexico depended on the rains for their agriculture, and the importance of water is reflected in the names of their deities: First Woman or Caha Paluna is "Falling Water," Ix Kan Itzam Thul is "She, the Precious Witch of the Gushing Water," Ix Puxyola is "She, the Destroyer of the Heart of Water," and Ix Tan Yol Ha is "She Who is in the Heart of the Showery Water."

The Aztecs in the highlands of central Mexico also honoured a water goddess. She was called Chalchihuitlicue, Mistress of the Rains and Waters, and she ruled during a time of chaos and disharmony called the Fourth Sun. Chalchihuitlicue sent a great flood to drown the disobedient people, but saved a chosen few and built them a rainbow bridge to the light of the Fifth Sun. Their descendants always remember her rage as well as her mercy, and make annual pilgrimages to her temple, where they pray to her to send just enough water for the crops.

THE NORNS

Guardians of the Sacred Waters

The trinity of Nordic deities in Icelandic legend is called the Fates, or the Wyrd Sisters. The eldest, Urth, or Mother Earth, is the creator who lives in a cave at the source of the Fountain of Life, called Urdarbrunnr or Stream of Urd. The bubbling magical waters of this sacred well were used each day by the Norns to water Yggdrasil, the World Tree, which linked the earth and the heavens. Norse mythology held that a serpent constantly gnawed at the roots of this monumental ash tree, and that one day it would fall, destroying the universe. This was the gathering place of the gods, who came here every day over the rainbow bridge but who were helpless to act without first receiving the wisdom of the Urdarbrunnr.

Urth's second sister, Vertandi, is the protector of motherhood as well as ruler of the phases of the moon. The third sister, Skuld, is known as the Death Norn, who laid a doomsday curse on the whole universe; her name is immortalized in the words *skulduggery* and *scold*. These three goddess sisters carried all the wisdom of the world. They knew the past, present and future of every person, and pronounced the fate and destiny of each child at birth.

Detail of oil and wind on water, Iceland, 1992. Mother Earth uses the waters of the Fountain of Life to nourish Yggdrasil, the World Tree of the Norse.

SEQUANA

Goddess of the Seine

The feminine deities of the Celtic and later the Roman culture pervade the area of present-day France that was once called Gaul. Sacred wells, springs and rivers were powerful symbols of fertility and the focus of Celtic ritual. Even the earth goddesses were perceived as flowing water, seen not in the landscape itself but in the water that drained it. Sequana was the protectress of the Seine River and its many adjacent valleys, and her temple shrine marked the spring at the source of the river. An ancient bronze plaque found here portrays the goddess surrounded by cornucopias and fertility symbols, being drawn down the river in a vessel shaped like a duck. Votive offerings and small statues were thrown into the water perhaps to ensure her beneficence to her people, the Sequana tribe. In 1963, during an excavation of the marshland near the source of the Seine, more than 140 oak-carved figurines were found deeply embedded under a blanket of vegetation, which had preserved these ancient gifts to the Goddess.

Other goddesses are also immortalized in the waterways of ancient Gaul. The Marne River took its name from the Mother Goddess, Matrona, whose secret rites were celebrated only by women. Melusine, daughter of the Celtic water goddess Pressina, is still honoured with serpent-shaped cakes at festivals celebrating her annual feast day in the town of Poitiers. The seven underground streams flowing deep beneath the cathedral of Notre Dame (Our Mother) at Chartres are powerful reminders of the mother goddess known to have been worshipped for thousands of years at this ancient goddess site.

Triple exposure of Claude Monet's water garden by the Seine, Giverny, France, 1995. Water spirits such as Sequana were a focus of Celtic ritual.

VULTURE WIFE and UNDERWATER WOMAN

Magical Shamans of Angel Falls

Auyan Tepui and Angel Falls, Canaima National Park, Venezuela, 1990. Vulture Wife loses her husband, Maichak, who flees to Auyan Tepui.

Vulture Wife was the shape-shifter of the Camaracota tribe, who lives near Angel Falls in northern Venezuela. Vulture Wife transformed herself into a beautiful woman and lured the tribal hero Maichak to be her husband, thereby giving him the chance to acquire the animal spirit power he desired. He succeeded in the three tests imposed by her chieftain father before they married, in the process acquiring too much power and the knowledge that the chieftain had two heads, a secret known only to Vulture Wife. The chief was terrified and ordered the vultures to kill Maichak, who fled the village but was trapped on Auyan Tepui, the massive rock summit of Angel Falls. Unable to descend, he was rescued by a lizard spirit who carried him down, and Maichak returned home still full of the wisdom gained from this dangerous liaison with Vulture Woman, a powerful feminine force.

Underwater Woman, a shamanic deity of the Orinoco tribe, who lives below Angel Falls, enticed men to her home and taught them how to cope with the chief of the malevolent water spirits. One story tells of a man who was searching for supernatural powers under the water. He ignored the advice of Underwater Woman, betrayed the water spirits, and was killed by the chief, an anaconda serpent who rose into the sky in the form of a rainbow. Today, local lore warns that approaching the base of the falls may cause sickness and death, especially if one looks at the rainbow.

Red sap in stream near Angel Falls, Canaima National Park, Venezuela, 1990. Canaima, jungle goddess of the Camaracota Indians, swallows everything in her path.

OUR MOTHER

Ruler of Eternal Water

The indigenous Guarani people of Paraguay have
a powerful myth about a female deity who rules
in an earthly paradise, a land without evil known as
Iva Mara Ei. It is said that when pilgrims arrive at the
house of Our Mother they are met by a parrot who
offers them food but also judges them, admitting
only those who are truly humble. The Guarani people
say that Our Mother lives in the land of eternal water
to the east. Guarani shamans have directed frequent
Messianic migrations toward this paradise, encouraging their people to escape the political and social
oppression they have endured over hundreds of years
of colonial rule.

Iguassu Falls at the junction of Paraguay,
Uruguay and Brazil, 1995. Our Mother lives
in Iva Mara Ei, land of eternal water.

NYI RORO KIDUL

Goddess of the South Seas

Java Sea from Indonesian coast, seen through fish-eye lens, 1989. Nyi Roro Kidul taught the king about the power of the spirits, and warned his people of the hidden forces under the ocean.

Nyi Roro Kidul, the daughter of an ancient king, was banished from her father's home by a wicked step-mother. Grieving, she threw herself into the ocean and became the Goddess of the South Seas. Eventually Nyi Roro Kidul left her palace under the sea to marry the King of Java, bestowing her divine powers on the royal family. Today, traditional beliefs still prevent people from swimming off the south shore of Java, where it is said that Nyi Roro Kidul seduces young men.

Open lava tube, Kilauea, Hawaii, 1987. Pele erupts as fire from deep within the earth.

TRANSFORMATION

The Wild Psyche

By putting ego aside and allowing the darkness of the shadow to surface in the psyche, we are able to live in our fullest capacity. Only when the depths of chaos, despair and death are recalled and integrated does the soul emerge into the illumination of understanding and enlightenment. The archetypal feminine journey taken by the soul through the shadow side of life is often a tortuous descent into darkness, wending through labyrinthine passages that lack a visible exit and are fraught with danger and magical occurrences. In fact, the soul often needs to be rescued or to bargain for its release. Sometimes guides appear in the form of demons who taunt or seduce. Others come in disguises such as the ugly hag who transforms into a beautiful goddess or bejewelled queen, or the mysterious, dark crone who directs her followers to a wise choice at the crossroads of life. The goddess of transition has faced her shadows and grown into the power that comes with wisdom, enabling her to lead us into the creativity and spontaneity of an authentic life.

This journey is one of completion, rebirth and integration of all aspects of the self, thus allowing the soul to express its full power and joy in life. It is the ultimate promise of transcendence, not through rising above the physical self but through being rooted in the earthy depths of the darkness. It is the experience of the deep eroticism and wisdom of the dark goddess that anchors all aspects of the self, giving access to the lightness of life. Finally, like the gold of the alchemists, we will be transformed into our highest state and allowed to live in the fullness of our being.

THE BLACK MADONNA

Lady of the Crypt

Chartres Cathedral in France is a spectacular twelfth-century monument to medieval Christian devotion. Like many other Christian sites in Europe, the church was built over a grotto that was a Celtic sanctuary where Druids worshipped the statue of "virginis pariturae," the virgin about to give birth. In AD 44, Christian missionaries converted the Druids and built the church dedicated to Notre Dame, Our Lady.

The crypt of the contemporary cathedral encloses the ancient grotto that now shelters a statue of the Black Madonna and Child. Faded frescos on the walls and star designs on the ceilings flicker in the dim light. These ancient paintings are reminders of the cult of Isis or Au Set, Mother Goddess of Egypt, whose story is echoed in many Christian tales. The goddess still reigns in this mysterious cavern in the belly of the earth. In this subterranean darkness is the shadow side of life – the earthy, hidden part of the feminine self that is often experienced in fear, sexuality and death. These are the transformative forces that are so frequently the author of deep soul experiences. But not all evidence of the ancient goddess is hidden: the two spires of the main cathedral entrance are crowned with symbols of the Earth Mother, one with a sun and the other with a moon.

Painting on curved ceiling of the crypt, Chartres Cathedral, 1995. The Black Madonna is surrounded by stars, symbols of the ancient goddess Isis. (below) Virgin of the Crypt, the Black Madonna is hidden in the crypt below the nave, close to the confluence of seven underground streams.

LILITH

Spirit of Revenge

This goddess of many ancient Middle Eastern tribes was known by a variety of names, including Belit-ili to the Sumerians and Baalat, the Divine Lady, to the Canaanites. The Old Testament names her as a screech owl, reminiscent of the ancient bird goddess, as well as Inanna and Ishtar, who were called Divine Lady Owl. The Talmud describes Lilith as a charming woman, the Kabbalah says she taught wisdom to Adam and other texts suggest that she was created first or that she was equal to him. She is probably best known as Adam's rebellious first wife, the woman who refused him when he tried to control their lovemaking and who then used her magical powers to discover the secret name of Jehovah. Lilith also demanded that Jehovah give her power over the winds, and she flew away (similar to the winged Isis and the other ancient bird goddesses) to the Western Desert, where she indulged in orgies with elemental spirits and sand demons. But the Hebrew nation was not rid of her; Lilith returned nightly to tempt Adam after his sin with Eve was punished with a penance of no sexual intercourse for a century.

Hebrew texts dating from as early as 2400 BC also talk of the night monster who haunted the ancient tribe of Edom, tickling the feet of babes and strangling them in their cradles. The power of this tale still strikes terror in the hearts of some Jewish families: mothers who witness their sleeping infants smiling or laughing will tap the baby's nose three times and tell Lilith to go away. Orthodox Jewish homes often have an image of Lilith turned to the wall to negate her seductive powers. The Zohar, the mystical texts compiled in the thirteenth century, names her as the "ruin of the world." During the witch hunts of late medieval times, women were tortured and killed after being accused of killing infants, copulating with demons and seducing men – sins historically attributed to Lilith.

Rock formations, Petra, Jordan, 1989. Lilith indulged in orgies with elemental spirits and sand demons.

KALI

Goddess of Eternal Time

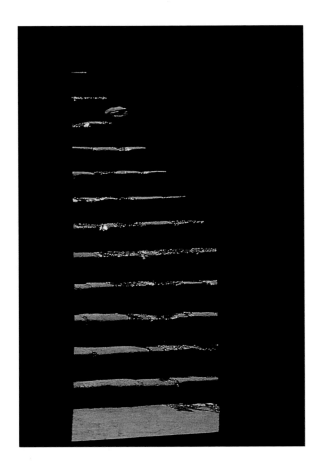

Steps into Temple of Kali, Benares, India, 1989.
Kali leads us through the shadows so that we may see
our wholeness.

As the Hindu symbol of eternal time, Kali is often misunderstood in her role as a goddess of death. As a spiritual symbol she embodies all our fears and terror of being destroyed. In her blackness, all distinctions disappear and eternal truths are realized. Kali's necklace of skulls gives testimony to her wisdom, as her bloody sword cuts through the illusions of life, forcing us to face our mortality. The name of Calcutta, her temple city, is derived from the Anglicization of Kali-Ghat, meaning "steps of Kali." The paradox of life can be seen in her temple, where death and suffering are tempered by the loving ministrations of the Sisters of Charity, founded by Mother Teresa.

As Shakti of the great god Shiva, Kali is the animating energy that allows him to unleash his power. Once we face the fullness of her wild, uncontrolled energy, she frees us from all fear and comforts us through eternity. In this way Kali is perhaps the most powerful of the dark goddesses, assisting us to see that which is hidden inside us and in the world around us, illuminating for a moment the shadowy parts of our existence. By showing us death, Kali gives us the knowledge and power to live out the authentic fullness of existence.

Stormy sky, 1986. Kali's wild, uncontrolled energy is seen in the blackness of space.

*Time exposure of lightning storm, 1997. Oya, the
goddess of winds and tornadoes, harnesses the
lightning to the earth.*

OYA

Whirlwind of Darkness

For the Yoruba culture of Nigeria, the feminine voice
in mythology is the power that connects people to
the divine. Oya is the goddess of winds, tornadoes
and lightning; in some legends she is called Buffalo
Woman and is known as the red woman who came
from a foreign land. Oya has had a strong influence
on Afro-American goddess traditions, and she is
an important Orisa (deity) in the Brazilian religion
Macumba, in which she is portrayed holding a flame
that symbolizes her ability to speak with the fire of
truth.

In Nigeria, Oya is personified as a whirling torna-
do with lightning piercing the blackness of cosmic
space. Like the other dark goddesses, she reveals what
is hidden, forcing us to acknowledge and address the
boundary between life and death. Oya carries a beaded
horsetail called the Irukere, which is a symbol of her
ability to ride the horse of sexual passion, connecting
her followers with sexual prowess and deep eroticisim.
Like Kali, she wields a sword of wisdom that cuts
through the illusions of this life. Like the Shaktis of the
Hindu tradition, Oya provides an energizing force to
the gods, who are powerless without her. Oya is alternately known as the wife or sister of Shango, the storm
god, to whom she gave the power of lightning.

INANNA

Mesopotamian
Queen of Heaven

The Sumerian goddess Inanna and her later
Babylonian counterpart, Ishtar, offer us the
earliest illustrations of the archetypal feminine journey to the underworld to confront and reclaim the
shadow side of life. According to a story dating from
3000 BC, Inanna leaves her temple of gold and lapis to
descend through the seven gates, at each level giving
up a symbol of her royal status as the demons of the
underworld taunt her. Her moon crown, earrings,
rings, gilded sceptre, girdle jewelled with the zodiac,
rainbow necklace and heavenly robe are all discarded,
and she is forced naked into the underworld. Here
she meets her dark twin sister Ereshkigal, Goddess
of Death, who impales her on a post for three
days. Inanna is rescued by her faithful companion
Ninshubur, Queen of the East, who begs Enki, the
god of wisdom, to intercede and bargain with the
Queen of the Underworld to release Inanna and let
Inanna's consort Dumuzzi take the goddess's place for
half of the year. Inanna is then reborn and, like the
waxing moon, regains her radiance as she ascends out
of the darkness to return to her queenly duties.

    Source of the earth's fertility, Inanna is called the
"Amazement of the Land," as she fills the rivers, springs
and wells with her waters. As the goddess of love and
desire, she is known as the Opener of the Womb, who
teaches her priestesses ancient love rituals in her temple city of Uruk in Mesopotamia. Here she re-enacts
the annual *heiros gamos* (sacred marriage), the ritual sexual union with her consort that maintains the eternal
unions of moon and sun, heaven and earth, and the
cycle of the seasons.

*Agitated water on
surface of river,
refraction filter,
1989. Inanna, the
Queen of Heaven,
wears a rainbow
necklace and is
crowned with
the stars.*

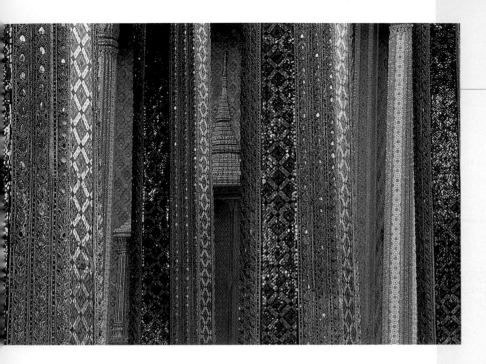

YESHE KHADOMA

Goddess of Hidden Knowledge

Sequinned pillars and portal, Emerald Buddha Temple, Bangkok, Thailand, 1990. The Khadoma Queen rules the Tantric deities from her enchanted castle hidden in the forest. (below) Dew on backlit grasses with refraction filter, 1985.

This compassionate being is Queen of the Khadomas, the fairylike Tantric deities who display many magical and occult powers. The Khadomas live in Bardo, the astral plane, where they pass on occult powers or assist their followers with difficult rituals. In one story where she is disguised as a beggar, Yeshe Khadoma utters a word unknown to Tilopa, the philosopher and holy man. The wise man is puzzled, and his curiosity leads him on an arduous journey following the beggar woman through the land of the Dakinis, the sky-walkers or priestesses of Tantric tradition who tend the dying. Tilopa discovers her in a cemetery, where she tells him to seek out the Tantric queen. He continues his quest, struggling on many blind paths through wilderness and forest until finally he discovers Yeshe Khadoma on a jewelled throne in her enchanted castle.

KURA NGAITUKA

Bird Woman of the Maori

Mineral springs, Rotorua, New Zealand, 1987. Bird Woman tried to retrieve her power objects but died in the hot springs of Rotorua.

The gigantic Maori goddess Kura Ngaituka is one of many mysterious forest creatures who do not have fire, so she uses her spearlike nails to tear at her uncooked food. Her feathery wings and pointed lips help her to impale birds, which she collects in her cave. Kura Ngaituka also captured the hero Hatupatu, to keep as her pet. One day while she was away, Hatupatu killed her guard birds, destroyed all her *tapu*, or ceremonial places, and escaped from the cave with her weapons and feathers. However, one of her birds escaped and warned Kura Ngaituka of this desecration. She raced after Hatupatu to reclaim her power objects, but she died in the steamy mineral springs of Rotorua, a place sacred to the indigenous people of New Zealand.

The goddess in the form of a bird is found in many ancient cultures, one of the earliest being the bird-woman figure in the Lascaux caves of Paleolithic France, dating from 20,000 BC. Bird-masked female figures were prominent in ancient Europe, Turkey and Crete. The stork, owl, raven, eagle and dove are intercessors in various world legends, where birds act as messengers between heaven and earth, bringing omens, communicating with angels or carrying souls. The bird as a symbol of expanded consciousness is often described in trance journeys, which usually begin with the shaman taking on a bird form and flying up or diving down. Birds are also special because they are twice born, first in the egg and then out of it. Maori myths relate how one bird was taught a chant for a successful sweet potato crop, and how another messenger bird learned its destination after a charm was repeated over the bird.

PELE

Goddess of Volcanic Fire

Solidified lava, Volcanoes National Park, Big Island, Hawaii, 1983. Pele creates new land as her lava cools.

As a young girl, Pele was fascinated by fire and once caused a conflagration in her homeland. Knowing she would cause more trouble, her mother, Haumea, the Earth Goddess of Polynesia and Mother of Hawaii, sent Pele and several of her sisters to Hawaii. At that time Hawaii was only a small atoll, so Pele used her powers of divination to choose good places to build islands. However, another sister, Namaka, the ocean goddess, followed her and attacked Pele for causing such destruction at home. Pele then became a disembodied spirit and disappeared into the volcano, where the Hawaiians honour her as earthly fire.

Pele has many guises: she is seen as a beautiful woman who seduces her admirers into the inferno of desire and darkness, and as a wizened old woman who talks to people and disappears in the middle of the conversation. She lives deep in the darkness of the earth, emerging into the world as a fiery eruption. Her wrath is appeased by offerings thrown into her craters or by bottles of gin left beneath the red blossoms of the Ohia tree on the slopes of Mauna Kea, the volcanic mountain on the Big Island of Hawaii. In the fire of her favourite haunt, the volcano of Kilauea, she is the force of destruction, her fiery lava swallowing the trees in her path. She is also a creative force, for when the lava flow cools, it solidifies to make new land.

Of the thousands of people who visit Volcanoes National Park each year, those who ignore the warnings not to remove lava rocks are said to pay the price of devastating changes in their lives. Every day, rocks are returned to park headquarters with messages of contrition.

Flowing lava, Volcanoes National Park, Big Island, Hawaii, 1983.
Pele's fires destroy everything in her path.

Detail of opal rock, Australia, 1989. Birra-nulu was attached to a crystal rock and petrified in place.

BIRRA-NULU

Mother of All

Birra-nulu is the creation goddess of the Aboriginals of southeastern Australia. Her husband, Baiame, is the Great Spirit and is entrusted with the sacred knowledge of the Father Spirit. Baiame elevated Birra-nulu to the position of Mother of All, allowing her to live with him in the sky. Like Baiame, Birra-nulu has a totem for each part of her body, so all the tribes can claim her as their own.

However, Birra-nulu was not always reliable and mature. One day she and her friend Kunan-beila, another wife of Baiame, were left alone while he was away hunting. While they were gathering food in the desert heat, they decided to swim in the spring at Coorigil, even though Baiame had warned them not to. The Kurrias, crocodile guardians of the pool, quickly swallowed them and disappeared. Baiame finally rescued them and brought them to his home in the Milky Way, where he attached them to a crystal and allowed them to petrify as a reminder of his time on earth.

OLD WOMAN

Bringer of Death

The valley of the Milk River in southern Alberta has been free of glaciation for more than fifty-five thousand years. This vent in the Earth Mother is believed to have been a migratory path for many ancestral clans moving through the North American continent. This is sacred land to the Blackfoot people, whose young men still seek spiritual guidance through vision quests in the Sweetgrass Hills, to the south. Nearby is Aysin'eep, the place called Writing-On-Stone, which has pictographs and petroglyphs that legends say were made by the spirits. Paintings and carvings of shamanic figures, vulvas, birds, animals and people are nestled on rock faces between hoodoos, the sandstone columns formed by wind and water. Some rocks in the valley are covered with carvings of headless human torsos that seem like spirits emerging out of the living rock.

This is the home of Old Man, or Napi, the Blackfoot creator who felt something was missing in the world he made. For four days he fashioned various rough and misshapen figures from clay. When he was finally satisfied with his creations, he covered them for four more days until he saw signs of life. An old woman and child then emerged and followed him to

Milk River, hoodoos and Sweetgrass Hills,
Writing-On-Stone Provincial Park, Alberta, 1997.
Old Woman's stone sank in the river, confirming her
choice that death would now be part of life.

the river, where he gave them the power of speech and explained life to them. Old Woman asked if they would always be alive, but Napi did not know. So he suggested they ask for an answer by floating a buffalo chip in the water, and if it sank, then death would occur. Old Woman disagreed, saying a buffalo chip would disintegrate, so she decided to use a rock. She threw a rock in the river, and as it sank, Old Man declared that her choice meant that people would die.

Multiple exposure with zoom lens movement on landscape and sculpture, 1996. Hekate meets her followers at the tri via, *where three paths converge and choices must be made.*

HEKATE

Queen of the Night

As a moon goddess of darkness and magic, Hekate is the protectress of Greek women when they leave their homes. This crone deity has integrated her life experience, incorporating the virgin and mother aspects to allow her to use her wisdom and prophetic knowledge in a powerful way. She meets her devotees at the *tri via*, "the three ways," which is the convergence of three roads where one path ends and new choices must be made. Hekate exemplifies crone energy at its greatest intensity, teaching her initiates that when the old dies, regenerative growth occurs and allows the shift into a new aspect of personal authenticity.

Our contemporary Western attitudes often devalue the power of the crone. While women elders are highly valued in most indigenous cultures, North American and western European cultures idolize youth and beauty. The skills and experience of older women are often underutilized, ignored or trivialized, as portrayed in the comic version of a "bag lady." Unfortunately, many women who perceive themselves only as grey-haired grandmothers perpetuate this diminished view of the crone. Perhaps we need to turn to Hekate to relearn the power of the *tri via*.

DZONOKWA

Woman of the Woods

Dzonokwa is a giantess of the Nootka and Kwakiutl tribes of the northwest coast of Canada. Dzonokwa is associated with copper, which is highly valued for its brilliance and malleability. As a symbol of abundance, Dzonokwa is called upon in potlatch ceremonies, which are central to the distribution of wealth and the spiritual renewal of the community. She is also said to capture and eat children, who are cautioned to stay close to home when they hear her voice in the hoot of the owl. This legend still operates in popular belief when a person about to die says, "I heard the owl call my name."

Although many stories revolve around the fearful and threatening forms of Dzonokwa, she is also considered to be a transformer. When her son was accidentally killed by hunters, for example, she was left alone, grieving by the sea. A lonely young man, an ugly orphan, came to her aid and used his canoe to bring her dead son's body back to shore. After she revived her son with magical water, Dzonokwa threw some on the ugly boy, transforming him into a handsome man. She taught him her secrets of rebirth and gave him riches and a mask of her face that contained her powers. He then returned to his village, revived his own parents with the magic, and shared his bounty with his friends and family.

Rainbow kelp and sea cave, Vancouver Island, 1996. Dzonokwa, the goddess of abundance, grieves alone by the sea after her son is killed.

ARTEMIS-DIANA

Goddess of the Moon

Double exposure of lunar eclipse and night landscape, 1988. As the moon goddess, Artemis-Diana brings light to the dark journey of the night.

Artemis, who is the virgin moon goddess, is often depicted as a fleet huntress running through the forest and protecting the animals, for which she was called Lady of the Beasts. In ancient times, popular festivals devoted to Artemis involved rituals under the full moon, where orgiastic dancing and spontaneous mating testified to her wild energy.

In the legendary goddess-worshipping colonies of Amazons that reached as far as Cappadocia (southern Turkey), Libya and northern Greece, women were renowned for their physical prowess and romantic love for each other. Their devotion was recorded in temples dedicated to Artemis and in the poetry of Sappho, who resided in the sacred colony on the island of Lesbos. Rituals at the temple at Brauron, near Athens, celebrated Artemis in the festival of the bear, one of her popular manifestations. According to myth, sacrifices of men and animals were made to appease her. As the She-Bear, the constellation Ursa Major, Artemis ruled the movement of the stars around the Pole Star, thereby determining the months and the seasons. The Helvetians proclaimed her as the She-Bear and named the city of Berne after her, and the Celts called her Artio and linked her with the bear king, Arthur. The Saxons called her Ursel, She-Bear; the Christians later canonized her as Saint Ursula. As the Anatolian Mother Goddess, Artemis reigned in a later manifestation under the Roman name of Diana and as Goddess Anna or Dea Anna. At the Temple of Ephesus, one of the Seven Wonders of the World, statuary adorned with multiple breasts depicts her fertility role. Her name is immortalized in the herb artemisia, where her power is employed to ease the pains of childbirth.

THE ELBOWS
SHARPENED
WOMEN

Hags of the Lodge

Red ochre pictograph, Hickson Lake, Saskatchewan,
1997. The Elbows Sharpened Women were one of
many obstacles Ayas dealt with on his quest to
find his mother.

The Cree people of northern Saskatchewan live in the
Canadian Shield, a rocky forested land penetrated by
many lakes and rivers. These remote lakes, accessible
only by canoe, were often the sites of vision quests,
where a young man would spend days by himself in
search of his spirit guide. On Hickson Lake, called
Masinaso-ee, a series of red ochre pictographs are
painted on the stone just above the water line. One is
a female figure with her elbows extended into knife-
like projections.

Although the meaning of these pictures is not well
understood, one Cree legend may account for these
women as agents of transformation. The story tells of a
boy, Ayas, who went in search of his mother. He and his
mother had been abandoned by his grandfather, who
had left them at the mercy of a giant snake believed to
be a spirit guardian who required a sacrifice. Ayas's
quest was full of danger, but he relied on spirit beings
to help him. In one village, he visited the tipi of two
blind old women called Okinipocoskwanisiwak, "the
ladies with sharpened elbows." But Ayas had been
warned by his grandmother that these old women

intended to stab him, so he left by the other side of the
tent. Hearing him leave, the old women started stab-
bing with their elbows and killed each other. Ayas was
then able to continue on his quest, and after many
more trials he was finally reunited with his mother.

MENILY

Moon Maiden of the Cahuilla

Palm Canyon, near Palm Springs, California, 1996. Menily, the Moon Maiden, grew sickly and wanted to run away.

According to the creation story of the Cahuilla people of the California desert, the original beings are called *nukatem*. They embodied the creative power of the universe. Eventually these original beings stopped being active and turned into the moon, stars, rainbows and other objects in the natural world. Now all people and things are related because they all contain this original creative power.

Menily, the Moon Maiden, was one of very few female *nukatem*, a beautiful young woman who taught the people how to play games, dance and have fun. She took the women and girls to bathe in secluded pools before the men got up, and as the sun rose, she showed them how to shake out their long hair so it would not tangle.

Cahuilla legend states that one night the creator god Mukat "made trouble" with Menily, leaving her sad and sickly and wanting to run away. She created a song to tell her people what happened, and then used her powers to make them sleepy as she disappeared into the sky. When the people awoke, they searched everywhere, but even Coyote could not find her, until one night they saw her in the pool, laughing at them. They begged her to come out, but she refused. Coyote drank most of the water, but still Menily would not come up from the pool. Finally they looked up and saw her in the sky, at the time of the new moon.

Multiple exposure and zoom lens movement on Washingtonia palm trees,
Palm Canyon, near Palm Springs, California, 1996. Menily taught the
women how to shake out their long hair so it would not tangle.

Glacial ice, Greenland, 1992. Sila controls storms from her home under the sea.

INTEGRATION

The Healing Spirit

Cultures around the world have long celebrated the healing power of the goddess. Embodying the qualities of nurturance, protection, love, joy, renewal and abundance, this goddess of harmony integrates body, soul and spirit. She is the vehicle to personal authenticity, restoring us to wholeness by healing the dualities and darkness that separate us from our core being. She incorporates the earthy, sexual, emotional and hidden aspects of our lives, and allows us to continue on the soul-making paths that lead us to our wisdom.

These healing deities provide us with sanctuary, guidance and compassion. They unify earthly and heavenly paradise and embrace us with the light of the universe. They may restore tribal harmony, access immortality, diminish pain and suffering, or provide pleasures of the senses. All these goddesses offer renewal, healing and salvation as we continue on our quest to uncover our deepest essence.

MARY

Virgin of the Rose

Notre Dame, Chartres, France, 1995. The ancient labyrinth was constructed as a symbol of the pilgrimage through life.

The immense Romanesque and Gothic structure of Chartres Cathedral is called Notre Dame, Our Lady, and is the home of the Virgin Mary. The light reflected through more than 160 stained glass windows is said to be the healing glow of God; the north window portrays Mary with four doves, symbols of the Holy Spirit and of the ancient bird goddess. Here, she is honoured for bringing salvation to the world by birthing the Christ child. As the intercessor between humankind and God, Mary is said to be the temple, the image of paradise and the queen of the kingdom of heaven. In the candle-lit sanctuary of the Madonna of the Pillar, a black statue adorned in queenly attire is elevated on a straight black post, not unlike the ancient tree of the goddess Asherah. The soaring ceiling of the Gothic nave that embraces Mary has been likened to a forest in stone, reminiscent of the grove of the ancient goddess.

Medieval pilgrims would have gathered inside the south entrance, where a labyrinth is emblazoned on the floor. Like the first labyrinth built by Daedalus in Minoan Crete, this mandala symbolizes the journey of the soul through life; the circular path culminates at the six-lobed central rose, an ancient goddess symbol particularly associated with Aphrodite, Isis and Mary. In medieval belief, the labyrinth was seen as the road to salvation and the way of the Crusaders, and its path, 203 metres (666 feet) long, was often used as penance to allow seekers to experience the difficulty in reaching the heavenly Jerusalem. Some contemporary visitors who explore the statuary and study the stained glass do not even notice the labyrinth, which tour guides seem to relegate to pagan mysticism rather than acknowledging it as a major integrating symbol in the cathedral. In fact, the pattern is almost completely covered with rows of wooden chairs laced together so they cannot be moved. At the summer solstice, devoted pilgrims walk through the labyrinth and watch as light from the south window converges on a paving stone in the floor nearby. This marking of the sun's rays on the longest day of the year echoes the cosmic measurements recorded in many pagan Celtic temples and monuments.

Time exposure of night sky, stars, moon and canyon walls seen through fish-eye lens, Petra, Jordan, 1989. The ancient bird goddess is reflected in the dove as a Christian symbol of the Holy Spirit appearing to the Virgin Mary.

Eucalyptus bark, Israel, 1989. Asherah was worshipped in the form of a living tree in the temple, a colourful reminder of her vibrant essence.

ASHERAH

The Living Tree

The name of the Canaanite goddess, Asherah, means "straight," a reference to her morality as well as to her manifestation in the form of an unshaped post or a living tree inside her temple. As the mother and nurturer of the gods, she was worshipped in groves of trees, and she was called upon at childbirth and during the planting of crops. Her full name was Lady Asherah of the Sea, although she was also called Elat, meaning "goddess."

The Old Testament forbade participation in the orgiastic rituals in celebration of Asherah's powers, despite widespread public worship by such prominent figures as Queen Maacah. Her daughter, Queen Jezebel, was killed by Hebrew zealots on the charge of harlotry during a festival of Asherah.

HATHOR

Divine Cow Mother

Detail of temple wall, Dendera, Egypt, 1988. Hathor wore the solar disc and horns of the bull, the sign of a powerful goddess.

The beloved goddess of Egypt ruled the underworld as well as the sky. Her many titles included Celestial Cow, Queen of Heaven, Queen of Earth, Goddess of Joy and Mother of Light. In her cosmic form as a winged cow she gave birth to the sun, and henceforth carried it between her horns as a symbol of her power. As a mother goddess, she adopted seven forms called the Hathors, the deities who foretold the destiny of children at birth as well as cared for the souls of the deceased. When she is enraged, Hathor is sometimes identified as Sekhmet, the goddess of war who assisted the sun god Ra to kill his enemies. She slaughtered so many people that Ra worried she would devastate the earth, so he mixed red dye with ale, which she drank, thinking it was blood. She then became intoxicated and forgot her mission.

Hathor's temples at Dendera and Thebes were honoured by worshippers for more than three millennia, even into historical times. Like the Greek goddess Aphrodite, Hathor and her followers revelled in music, the arts, dance and all sensuous pleasures of the body. The New Year's Festival at Dendera celebrated Hathor's birthday, when she was called Tanetu, Goddess of Light. Her image was removed from the temple and bathed in the rays of the early morning sun, signalling to her devotees to begin their revelry.

GUM LIN

Weaver of Bamboo

Bamboo forest, China, 1989. A thick forest provided Gum Lin with bamboo for her mats.

Long ago this Cantonese heroine wove bamboo mats to support her impoverished family, who lived in a desolate village that suffered drought for many years. She wandered far from home in search of bamboo, which she found in great abundance by a lake near the mountains. Gum Lin tried to make a channel to bring water to the poor villagers so they could grow rice, but she could not unlock the gate holding the river. Birds told her to find the daughter of the dragon, and a peacock folded its tail and directed her to Wild Swan Lake, where she found the dragon's daughter. Together they sang songs to lure the dragon from his lair, where Gum Lin found the key hidden in a box adorned with a swan. She opened the gate and watched the river flow to her village. Thenceforth Gum Lin was elevated to a deity, and even today villagers say they can hear the voices of two women singing in perfect harmony at Wild Swan River.

Just as the birds helped Gum Lin, a peacock also assisted Princess Po-i Ta Shi. This beloved Chinese deity is a manifestation of the Buddhist Goddess of Mercy, Kuan Yin, whose name means "earth" and "feminine flow." Po-i Ta Shi defied her father, the king, who demanded she marry and follow family tradition. Instead, she ran away to live in a Buddhist convent, the Temple of the White Bird, but her father found her and ordered that she be treated cruelly and be given the most difficult tasks. Po-i Ta Shi was helped by animals, including a peacock who used his feathery tail to sweep the kitchen floor. When her vengeful father eventually had her killed, she travelled to the underworld to end all pain and suffering in the world above.

Po-i Ta Shi is often portrayed holding a child, sitting on a lotus, completely covered with a white veil. It is this manifestation of Kuan Yin, the goddess of compassion "who hears the cries of the world," that is displayed as the Goddess of Democracy in contemporary demonstrations in China.

IXCHEL

Wife of the Sun

Known to the Maya as Lady Rainbow, Ixchel is the wife of the sun and consort of the creator god Itzamna. In her benevolent form she is the moon goddess as well as the protective patron of medicine, childbirth and weaving. From the tenth century until recent times, Ixchel's shrine on Cozumel, the Island of Swallows off the coast of the Yucatan Peninsula, was an important site where female worshippers came from the far-flung corners of the Mayan empire to pray for this island spirit to stir their wombs so they could bear a child.

A similar restorative nature is seen with Ixtab, the Mayan goddess of suicide, whose partially decomposed body hangs from a tree. Although her role as a death goddess sounds ominous, Ixtab provides her people with an honourable way to enter paradise. After a suicide, Ixtab takes the soul and lays it to rest beneath the World Tree, Yaxche, which, like the cosmic tree in many other cultures, contained the passageway to the hereafter.

Tree at shrine dedicated to Ixchel, Cozumel, Mexico, 1995. When people committed suicide, Ixtab laid their souls to rest beneath the World Tree, Yaxche.

GYHLDEPTIS

Spirit of the Cedar

Lichen on cedar boughs, Haida Gwaii, 1990. Gyhldeptis hangs from cedar trees, protecting the Haida from malevolent beings.

The only area of Canada that escaped the last ice age, the northwest coast rain forest supports a plethora of indigenous plants where the goddess Gyhldeptis, or Hanging Hair, can be seen draped on some of the oldest cedar trees in the world. For more than ten thousand years, her forest abode has provided the Haida with materials for baskets, blankets, clothing and food.

THE SULEVIAE

Guardians of the Well

As the mother guardians of the Gauls, these Celtic deities are found at shrines associated with healing waters in Britain and France. Today, local people still undertake an annual spring pilgrimage to Cloutie Well in northern Scotland, in honour of the Virgin Mary as well as the ancient deities. Chanting and praying on the journey through the forest to the holy well, pilgrims then leave strips of clothing on the nearby trees as a gift to the goddesses. This tradition dates from pagan times, when it was believed that as the cloth disintegrated, their ailment would be cured. This custom is similar to rituals at other sacred sites around the world, such as at the Bighorn Medicine Wheel in Wyoming, where Native Americans leave personal articles tied to the fence protecting the medicine wheel, thereby invoking the blessings of the spirits.

The Suleviae may be related to another water deity, Sulis, whose name has the same derivation as the Celtic words for "eye" and "sun." As the patron goddess of the thermal waters at Bath, England, Sulis was honoured into historic times by the Romans, who called her Minerva Medica, Goddess of Healing. The renown of the contemporary healing shrine to the Virgin Mary at Lourdes, France, is comparable to the importance of these sacred wells, found throughout the ancient Celtic world.

Cloutie Well, near Inverness, Scotland, 1995. The trees around sacred wells are draped with cloth offerings from pilgrims who hope to be healed.

SOPHIA

Virgin of Light

Multiple exposures on poplar grove, 1997. The light at the centre of creation is often manifested as a feminine deity.

The esoteric knowledge of many ancient cultures is stored in wisdom books that are used only by spiritual elders trained to deal with mystical questions. Many of these cultures portray the unknowable face of God as the light of the world, which is often personified in a feminine figure seen as a manifestation of nature.

The Shekinah is the Hebrew emanation of Yahweh, or God. Also known as the Bride of the Sabbath, the Shekinah is said to be the only tangible way to feel God with one's senses because she mani-fests herself as the light at the centre of all creation. The Shekinah is the garment of God seen in a radiant cascade of light over nature. Her robes and veils are the world as we know it. Like Shakti, the animating soul of the Hindu god Shiva, she is the activating energy that allows Yahweh to use his wisdom and creativity. The energy of the Shekinah is so far-reaching that she is sometimes called the Music of the Spheres, and her abundance is honoured in her title as Tree of Life, whose healing leaves are said to bear a different fruit each month.

Sophia is the Gnostic Great Mother, the Holy Spirit also known as Lady Wisdom. She is seen as the womb, the life-generating force that is embodied in all creation as the mirror of God, a reflection of eternal light. Some sacred texts compare her to Isis and Hathor, and speak of her as God's mother or the Virgin of Light, whose spirit entered Mary's body to conceive Jesus. Sophia is venerated as a saint by Eastern Orthodox Christians.

The Maid of Heaven is designated as God's messenger to the Baha'i prophet Baha'u'llah. The Maid appeared to Baha'u'llah as he lay in chains in the prison at Akka, and again in the Garden of Ridvan, where he resided before his death. Like Sophia, the Maid of Heaven also wears the Robe of Light as the embodiment of all creation that shines with the pleasure of God. She is alternately known as Beauty, Trustworthiness, and the Essence of Purity.

SEDNA

Inuit Mother of the Animals

The sea goddess Sedna is a provider as well as a healing
and integrating social force among the Inuit. Legend
says her father threw her out of their boat in an
attempt to calm the waters. She clung to the side until
he chopped off her fingers and she sank to the bottom.
Sedna now lives under the sea, where she controls the
food source. If she is angered by indiscretions in the
community, she will not release the animals to feed
her people, and the shaman must enter a trance and
travel to her home to unravel her hair, which will have
become tangled by the broken taboos.

   In some areas of the Arctic, Sedna manifests herself as the goddess Sila, the Majestic Woman, who controls storms from her home at the bottom of the sea.
As Ruler of All the Elements, she is the supreme deity
to whom prayers are directed. Storms, snow, rain and
sunshine are all messages from Sila.

*Water reflection, 1977. Sedna lives under the sea, where
she controls the source of food.*

Camera movement on moss-draped trees, the Himalayas, 1989. Souls in Bardo may be reborn through crevices in trees.

CHA-DOG-MA

Guardian of Bardo

The role of these Buddhist enlightened beings called Dakinis is to assist souls in their journey from life on earth to the astral plane called Bardo, the afterlife transition before entering another realm. There are many goddesses with various roles, such as Cha-dog-ma, who guards the west door, and Buddha Krotishaurima, the wrathful mother deity who brings blood in a shell. The inhabitants of Bardo may be dead, in deep meditation or in a trance state. Their bodies are exact replicas of the human body, with all of their senses and abilities intact. They live on ethereal essences of food given as offerings on earth, or from the harvest of the natural world. Some souls are elevated to the pure land called Shambhala, while others are reborn by falling through openings onto the earth or in trees, where they become ghosts or animal beings.

IDUNA

Love Goddess of the Norse

The Nordic peoples placed baskets of apples in graves to assist the souls of the dead to resurrect and transfer to another body. The Icelandic deity called Iduna, the Renewing One, is the goddess of the seasons who grew the golden apples of immortality in her magical garden in the west. She gave one apple to each deity of the sacred Aesir, the Norse gods led by Odin. Iduna's apple retained the youth and beauty of these gods, and then she made love to them. Once, Iduna and her apples were stolen by evil giants. The gods began to wither and grow old, like mere mortals. Only when she was rescued by the god Loki was their immortality restored.

Iduna also invented the runic alphabet, the stones used in divination, charms and curses. She engraved the characters of the runes on the tongue of her consort, giving him the magic of words, and he became the greatest of poets. However, this mystical knowledge was not available to other men until the great god Odin committed suicide by hanging himself on the sacred tree of Yggdrasil. This self-sacrifice was practised by other Norse heroes as the price of acquiring feminine wisdom.

Mosses on lower slopes of Snaefellsjokull, Iceland, 1992. The love goddess, Iduna, grew the apples of immortality in her garden in the west.

Mount Chimborazo, Ecuador, 1985. Mama Paccha lives in the form of a dragon beneath the mountain.

REVERENCE

The Mountain Dweller

Throughout history, the mountain has been conceived of as the abode of the sacred. As the place on earth closest to a heavenly paradise, it is said to be home to divine beings who communicate in both realms. Journeying up the mountain is seen as a spiritual quest in most cultural myths. A mountain peak is a place of connection and inspiration, the point of land furthest away from the profane concerns of earthly life. From this vantage point it is said one can see forever, penetrating the mists that veil the Other World.

Mountains are also traditionally considered to represent the Great Mother, with her breasts manifested in the cone-shaped hills and her rounded belly and pubic mound seen in the dips of valleys. Peaks of the Himalayas are named Goddess Mother of the Universe, Great Breast Full of Nourishment, and Blessed Goddess. The ancient mother goddess of Greece is called the Universal Mountain Mother, and Japan's Mount Fuji, Hawaii's Kilauea and the South American Andes are home to fiery, earth-shaking goddesses. Chinese mountains are the home of the Taoist immortals and Buddhist spirits. Celtic rituals often took place in mountain shrines, while on hilltops across Britain and Ireland the fires of Beltane were lit to honour the Earth Mother. For still other cultures, artificial mountains in the form of pyramids and ziggurats were built as thrones for the gods and often as high places to perform the ritual sacred marriage to the goddess. In this chapter, our journey continues to the peaks venerated through time as homes of the immortal mountain dwellers.

XI WANG MU

Goddess of the Immortals

This creator goddess lives on Kunlun, the dome in the middle of the Chinese mythical world. The sun and moon and all the universe revolves around this cosmic mountain. Before heaven and earth were created, legend says that this Taoist goddess was a peach tree in the Garden of Paradise, which nourished the universe. Now, as Goddess of Eternal Life, Xi Wang Mu tends the Peaches of Immortality in her mountain garden surrounded by the Lake of Pearls. She is the ruler of the fairies or legendary Immortals.

Western Mountains (above), and blossoms with light from garden lantern (below), China, 1989. The Taoist creator deity Xi Wang Mu lives on the cosmic mountain, where she tends the Peaches of Immortality.

FUCHI

Fire Goddess of Fujiyama

Female personification of volcanoes is echoed in many cultures: Pele (Hawaii), Mahuea (New Zealand), Aetna (Italy) and Chuginadak (Alaska). In the animist beliefs of the aboriginal Ainu people in Japan, Mount Fuji is the abode of the Fire Goddess, Fuchi. As one myth reveals, the god of nearby Mount Hakusan argued that his mountain was higher than Fujiyama, so the Buddha measured the height of the two peaks by connecting them with a pipe and pouring water down it. The water landed on the goddess Fuchi, thus proving his claim. Fuchi then displayed her anger and power by striking Mount Hakusan eight times, creating the eight peaks seen today.

Fuchi shares her home on Fujiyama with another guardian of the sacred mountain, Fuji Hime, the immortal Shinto princess who makes the trees bloom. Even today, Shinto pilgrims must cleanse and prepare themselves through ancient ceremonies before attempting the ritual ascent.

In addition to being the goddess of volcanic fires, Fuchi is also identified with two Ainu fire goddesses of the household hearth, Apemeru-ko-yan-mat, Fire Sparks Rise Woman, and Unameru-ko-yan-mat, Cinder Sparks Rise Woman. In these guises, Fuchi lives in every Ainu home, where all prayers are addressed through her.

*Mount Fuji and dewdrop, double exposure, Japan, 1989.
The Shinto fire goddess Fuchi shares her home on
Fujiyama with Fuji Hime, who makes the trees bloom.*

Sacred lake, Mount Batur and Mount Agung, from Penelokkan, Bali, 1989. The water goddesses live in the sacred lakes of Bali.

DEWI DANU
and DEWI BATUR

Deities of the Sacred Lake

In Bali, a mystical land of twenty thousand temples, Dewi Danu and other water goddesses are consulted to determine when and how crops are planted and irrigated. Indeed, recent computer studies show that the ancient methods of water control based on local shamanic traditions were highly sophisticated and successful techniques, yielding a much better crop compared to that from an experimental system using a government imposed planting schedule.

The Jero Gedé, the high priest of the water temple, was chosen as a young boy by Dewi Danu's priestess in a trance state. She then trained him in the ancient rites, which are an integral part of Balinese religion.

Another water goddess, Dewi Batur, lives in a sacred lake on Mount Agung, the abode of her husband, the god Agung. This peak, the highest of the Four Sacred Mountains, is the home of Bali's mother temple, Pura Besakih. The thousand-year-old Hindu temple complex contains more than thirty shrines, each dedicated to a Balinese clan descended from one of the eight traditional royal houses of Bali.

GOKARMO

Snow Goddess of the Himalayas

Himalayan range, Nepal, 1989. Gokarmo, or She in White Raiment, is the Shakti or animating energy of the Buddha.

As Mother Goddess of the fourth day of Bardo, Gokarmo enters the astral plain to protect the deceased souls. Gokarmo shares her Himalayan mountain home with Tsering Chhenga, the Tibetan Earth and Nature Mountain Spirits, who wear flowing robes and carry fertility symbols. These deities are the five sisters of Mount Everest, the grand mountain range the Tibetans call Chomo Lungma, meaning Mother Goddess of the Snows.

PARVATI

Daughter of the Himalayas

View of the Himalayas from Poon Hill, Gorepani, Nepal, 1989. Parvati, Earth Goddess and Daughter of the Himalayas, uses her supernatural powers to manifest herself in many guises.

Parvati, a manifestation of the great Indian Mother Goddess, Devi, personifies the Himalaya Mountains, where she rules the earth and nature spirits. As the consort and Shakti of the great god Shiva, Parvati provides the animating or energizing power that allows him to use his creative force. Her magical abilities so fascinated Shiva that he could not resist her, and he gave up his ascetic life to devote himself to sexually satisfying her until the world shook with their embracing. Parvati desperately wanted a child, but Shiva refused, instead ripping a piece of her skirt and telling her to fondle it. Dismayed, Parvati put the red cloth to her breast, whereupon a child took form and began to nurse. The angry and jealous Shiva beheaded the child but became contrite on seeing Parvati's grief. He then found the child an elephant's head, and that is why their son, the god Ganesha, is half human and half animal in form.

Myths say Shiva teased Parvati because she was dark-skinned (perhaps a reference to her origin in the ancient Dravidian culture, considered inferior by the caste-conscious Brahmans). Feeling unloved and ugly, Parvati escaped to her mountain retreat, where she practised yoga until the god Brahma granted her wish for golden skin. Now she appears with the skin of both colours and is sometimes worshipped as Gracious Uma, Mother Ambika, Good Wife Sati or Golden Gauri. At other times she manifests herself as the Goddess of Destruction in the form of Kali or Durga, the fierce, dark feminine deities who were also Shaktis to Shiva.

MAMA PACCHA

Mountain Earth Mother

As Mother Goddess of the Inca, Mama Paccha influenced many aspects of life. She was said to reside as a dragon beneath the Andes mountains, sending earthquakes along this backbone of South America. She taught her people to make corn beer, and she also manifests herself in other benevolent forms such as the spirit of night and day. The Quechua people around Cuzco believe she lives in the earth, where she controls agriculture; a special group of women in this tribe regard her as their companion and beseech her to provide them with a bountiful harvest. As the garden deity of tribes in northern Peru, Mama Paccha is honoured with corn meal offerings, and women talk to her while they plant and work in the fields.

Mount Chimborazo, Ecuador, 1985. Mama Paccha controls agriculture from her home in the earth.

MOOMBI

Clan Guardian of Mount Kenya

To the Kikuyu clans of central Kenya, the land is the core of their being and the legacy of the ancestors. From the time when the first Kikuyu chose a digging stick rather than a bow or spear, all Kikuyu people were considered children of the ancestral land. Moombi is the mother guardian of these clans, who make their home around Mount Kenya, the sacred mountain of mystery known to be the abode of the god Ngai. It is here that Moombi created the earth, which is considered a mother by these matrilineal people. Each village designates its own Mother, usually an elder woman, who is held responsible for the fertility of the earth. After a ritual blessing of the seeds, she harbours them in her hut in preparation for planting, to ensure a bountiful crop for these people, whose livelihood depends on the land.

Moon and vegetation, Mount Kenya, 1994. Moombi guards the clans of Mount Kenya, sacred mountain of Ngai.

GAIA

Prophetess of Mount Parnassus

A primeval prophetess of ancient Greece who is manifested as Earth herself, Gaia is the oldest deity on sacred Mount Parnassus. She was here before time began, when formless chaos settled into her deep-breasted shape to become Earth. In fact, Delphi, meaning "womb," the most sacred site in the shadow of Mount Parnassus, was originally a series of temples to Gaia. Only later was it redesignated by Zeus as the Omphalos, or navel of the world, and transformed into the sanctuary of Apollo. Below his sacred complex there remained a goddess shrine, and nearby temples were dedicated to Athena Pronoia, the classical Greek goddess who, as the patron of the city of Athens, was also enshrined in the Parthenon.

At Delphi, Gaia's vapours are said to seep from deep within her earthly womb to convey her wisdom to the Python, the oracle who straddles the sacred chasm on the slope of Mount Parnassus. Gaia was consulted throughout antiquity by the renowned of classical Greece, who came from afar to receive her prophetic direction on important matters.

Moonrise at Mount Parnassus and Temple of Athena through fish-eye lens, Delphi, Greece, 1989. Gaia's prophetic vapours seep up to the Python from deep within her earthly womb.

Clouds, with colour refraction filter, on the Yangtze River, China, 1989. The Cloud Princesses control weather patterns from their homes on the holy mountains of China.

NIANGNIANG

Princess of the Motley Clouds

Niangniang is the goddess of Tai Shan, the holy Buddhist mountain of central China. She is also known as Princess of the Motley Clouds, and is an ancient guardian of women and children.

Another cloud goddess is Bixia Yuanyin, a weather guardian known as Princess of the Purple and Azure Clouds. She also resides on Tai Shan, the sacred mountain of the east, where she is the ruler of the wind. Her sister goddess Yao Ji lives on Wu Shan, the sacred mountain near the Yangtze River. Yao Ji is also called the Turquoise Courtesan, as she presides over rain and fertility in her essence as the rainbow.

UMA

Light of Perception

Uma is a primordial being derived from Devi, the all-encompassing mother goddess of ancient India who ruled over all aspects of life and death. Uma is seen in the light that allows perception in the world, revealing the illusions of physical life on the earthly plain. She is also called the Gracious One when she is worshipped as an aspect of Parvati, the earth goddess. When she manifests herself as the crone aspect of Kali, Uma becomes the Shakti or animating power of the god Shiva. Uma can also be seen as a mountain ghost haunting the Himalayas, where she once lived with her sister Ganga, the goddess embodied in the sacred waters of the Ganges River.

Midday sun above clouds, photographed through plane window, 1985. Uma, the ghost of the Himalayas, provides light for us to perceive the world.

Sunset over Uluru (Ayers Rock), Australia, 1989. The mists of ochre powder decorating Wuriupranala's body cause red stains on the sunset clouds.

ILLUMINATION

The Sky Dancer

In most traditional cultures, the sky is a dwelling place of divine beings who travel between heaven and earth on a rainbow bridge. As the culmination of our journey, the images in this final chapter portray the goddesses who are personified in the elements of the cosmos. Embodied in the stars, moon, sun, clouds and aurora borealis, Sky Dancer travels the celestial realms, living in the promised light and the bliss of paradise. This deity takes the form of a dakini, an enlightened being of Tantric Buddhism, who has undergone many transitions and transformations to reach this spiritual peak. She has integrated all her earthly forms and can therefore fully experience her multidimensional self within the cosmic ether. Although we may regard Sky Dancer as totally free and spontaneous in her exploration beyond the constraints of earth, she is still a cosmic entity and must follow a set path that maintains her connection with the earth. In this way she remains part of the eternal pattern and rhythm of the universe.

The sky-dancing deity mirrors the ancient goddess in her form as a living tree. She is also a reflection of the mythological World Tree, with its roots deep in the earth and its branches stretching into the heavens. Despite being in a spiritually enlightened state, Sky Dancer is fully connected to her body, the vehicle for all sensual experiences, and can thus live erotically in the life-force that courses through her. She is the essence of reunited body, soul and spirit that is linked to the web of Spider Woman, the universal source of life that nourishes all beings.

Sky Dancer has completed her spiritual pilgrimage to the centre of the goddess's labyrinth and has blossomed into the fruits of her wholeness.

TARA

Queen of Time

As a form of Kali, Tara is a beautiful but self-combusting manifestation true to her name, which means "star." In Buddhism she is the feminine face of reality, propelling all life with her unquenchable hunger for release from the physical world. As the celestial boat woman, she ferries her people from the world of delusion to the world of knowledge. Tara is invoked under 108 names on the Buddhist rosary and is seen in five colours: green, blue, yellow, red and white. She is terrifying as the Green Tara but is the vehicle of enlightenment as the White Tara of meditation, known as the facilitator of many miracles.

Prayer flags at Buddha's cave, near Bodh Gaya, India, 1989.
Tara may be seen in five colours and invoked under 108 names.
(below) Star trails, 2-hour exposure, 1989. Tara, the star deity,
ferries her people to the world of knowledge.

ISHTAR

Moon Goddess of Babylonia

Waning eclipse of the moon, 1996. As the moon goddess Ishtar is reborn and retrieves her queenly attire, the moon regains her fullness and brilliance.

Known as "light-giving" in her role as the moon goddess, Ishtar, like her earlier Sumerian manifestation, Inanna, takes the ultimate mythic journey to experience death in the underworld. Ishtar sheds the symbols of her queenly attire at each of the seven gates and arrives naked in the underworld. She begs the death queen, Ereshkigal, to release her dead consort, Tammuz, the god of vegetation, so that he may be reborn to quiet the cries of the wailing women on the barren earth. When Tammuz is freed, Ishtar is reborn. She emerges through the gates of darkness, retrieving her queenly attire just as the waxing moon regains her brilliance, glowing in the sky to fulfill her position as Sharrat Shame, or Queen of Heaven.

Like Inanna and many other goddesses with both life-giving and death-bringing roles, Ishtar was also portrayed as the goddess of war, riding on a lion. As the nurturing aspect of the moon, she was called The Milky One. The Babylonians also personified Ishtar as the zodiac, picturing her within a circle of eight stars. On nights of the full moon, Ishtar's 180 temples in ancient Babylon celebrated this supreme goddess, whom they called by many names, including Mother of Deities, Ruler of the Heavens and Exalted One. In her great temple at Ninevah, near the Tigris River, priestesses and eunuch attendants prepared for the annual Akitu festival, where Ishtar re-enacted the sacred marriage. A shepherd boy chosen for his beauty and sexual prowess fulfilled his duty to the Queen and was then sacrificed in the name of Tammuz. This sacred coupling and Ishtar's ritual journey to redeem Tammuz from the underworld ensured her power to maintain the fertility of the earth, and renewed her honour as Glorious Lady of the Lands.

KANENE SKI AMAI YEHI

Cherokee Sun Stealer

One day, the people and the animals decided that they would get together and try to solve the problem of darkness. Badger, Possum and Buzzard all tried, but they failed to brighten the night. Finally Spider Grandmother proposed a solution, but the animals laughed at her. Undaunted, this crone called Kanene ski Amai yehi, fashioned a bowl of clay and started walking to the land of the Sun People, carefully spinning her web out behind her. Approaching the east, she crept close to the glow of orange and pinched a small piece into a bowl, then followed her thread home. As she walked, the fire in her bowl became so hot and bright that she could not hold it any longer, so she flung it into the sky, saving one small piece as a gift to the people for cooking.

Glow of sunrise on lake, through fish-eye lens, 1983. Spider Grandmother crept close to the glow of orange in the land of the Sun People.

NEITH and NUT

Creators of the Heavens

As the oldest of the Nile goddesses, Neith, who wears the crown of Lower Egypt, existed before time. In her role as Lady of the Starry Vault, she strung the sky on her loom and wove the world. She then spun nets to pull animal creatures and humans out of the chaos of the primordial waters. Finally she created childbirth and brought forth Ra, the powerful sun god.

In the complex pantheon of ancient Egypt, the goddess Nut is known as Mystery of the Heavens. As a sky goddess, she laid her body across the earth god Geb, her younger brother. Through this constant intercourse they parented the deities Osiris, Isis, Seth and Nephthys. The Sun God disapproved of this incest and directed the god Shu to separate them. Shu raised Nut's body into a great arch, holding up her star-spangled belly while her feet and fingers touched the earth. Nut's hair fell down like rain, and the Tree of Life grew at her feet. As Mother of Life, she births the sun every day, and as Goddess of Rebirth, she stands at both sides of the threshold between earth and the underworld.

Frieze of Nut on temple wall, Valley of the Queens, Egypt, 1988. Nut's body forms the stars arching over the earth.

!URISIS

African Sun Goddess

Sand dunes and acacia tree, Namib-Nauklift Park, Namibia, 1994. The sun goddess assists the hunter to stay in balance with his world.

The Bushmen and Hottentots of South Africa and Namibia are the earliest indigenous people still living in Africa. For the San Bushmen, the sun has a great voice. The sun goddess !Urisis makes a ringing sound in the sky to accompany and comfort the Bushmen in their nomadic lifestyle. !Urisis assists the Bushman hunter to stay in balance with his world; he feels he is in harmony as long as he can hear the ringing sound of the sun. !Urisis also dries the earth that cries for the rain to come. The Bushman woman sits by the fire and cries a lonely song, waiting for her hunter husband to return.

Shifting sands reveal buried thorn trees in parched lake bed at Dead Vlei,
Namib-Nauklift Park, Namibia, 1994. The sun goddess dries the earth
that cries for rain.

Double exposure of full moon and post-sunset light, Africa, 1995. Ol-apa wanted all her people to see her scars from her fights with Enk-ai.

OL-APA

Moon Goddess of the Masai

Ol-apa was married to Enk-ai, the sun god. Enk-ai was very embarrassed by the scars from their many fights, so he decided to become a bright light so the marks would not be seen. However, Ol-apa wanted everyone to see her cut mouth and missing eye, so she shines with less light. In her phase as the new moon, people throw a stone at her, requesting long life. Pregnant women put milk into a gourd covered with grass, pouring it in her direction to invoke Ol-apa's assistance for an easy birth. Both Ol-apa and Enk-ai now travel in the same direction. When she gets tired, he carries her for two days; then on the third day she is left where he sets, and by the fifth day she reappears to her people.

WURIUPRANALA

Aboriginal Sun Goddess

Before the world began, in a remote era known as the Dreamtime, the ancestral spirits of the Australian Aboriginals slept beneath the flat and unformed earth. These spirits eventually rose above the ground and shaped the landscape, singing it into existence and creating humans and teaching them how to survive. For this reason, the Aboriginals have a sacred trust with the land, which requires them to re-enact the Dreamtime rituals and sing the songs of the land to keep it alive.

Each morning, the sun goddess Wuriupranala makes a fire to light her torch of bark. The first dawn light is her fire, and the clouds of sunrise are reddened by dust from the powdered ochre that she uses to decorate her body. As the soft call of Tukumbini, the honey-eater bird, wakens the people, Wuriupranala travels all day with her blazing torch across the sky to the west. On that horizon she dips the torch into the ocean, her mists of ochre leaving red stains on the sunset clouds; then, using the glowing embers to light her way, Wuriupranala travels through the underworld back to her starting point in the east.

Sunset over Uluru (Ayers Rock), Australia, 1989. Wuriupranala uses the glowing embers to light her way through the underworld.

YESHE TSOGYEL

Sky Dancer

Backlit clouds over ridge, Annapurna Range, Nepal, 1989. The Sky Dancer, Yeshe Tsogyel, leads her followers on a mystical journey through Tantric sexual practices.

An eighth-century Tibetan princess and teacher, Yeshe Tsogyel was also the consort of Guru Rinpoche, the founder of Tibetan Buddhism. For many years she practised the mystical Tantric traditions in a cave high in the mountains of Tibet, where she acquired supernatural powers and attained spiritual perfection. Before leaving her body for the etheric realm, Yeshe Tsogyel promised to project a physical manifestation of herself in this place forever. As a Tantric Buddhist goddess, she became identified with the Dakini, or transcended deity, known as Victorious One of the Ocean of Wisdom. She is a vehicle to enlightenment who helps her devotees reach an elevated spiritual state through sacred sexual union. Her followers see Yeshe Tsogyel as the primordial female Buddha, a powerful guide to accessing their own inner wisdom.

The woman said to be a living projection of Yeshe Tsogyel now resides in a cave at an elevation of 6,000 metres (19,686 feet), in a valley called Shoto Terdrom, the Box of Treasures. Yeshe Tsogyel's emanation, called Tenzin Chodron, is elusive and magical, often appearing to her seekers in unrecognizable guises. It is said she can be seen flying over valleys and mountainous chasms, a sky dancer using her shawl like wings.

PANA

Weather Goddess of the Inuit

This deity of the Caribou and Palermuit Inuit people is known as the Woman Up There. She lives in the sky, where she cares for souls of the dead until they are ready to be reincarnated. Then Pana and the moon assist them to return to earth. The stars make Pana's home full of openings, and sometimes other things spill through the heavens in the form of rain, hail, snow and the aurora borealis.

Aurora borealis, stars, crescent moon and the comet Hale-Bopp, Saskatchewan, 1997. The stars, aurora borealis, moon and comet spill through from Pana's home in the heavens.

Setting sun and clouds, Allahabad, India, 1989. As the ancient mother goddess of the endless sky, Aditi existed before time itself and created the deities who rule the natural world.

ADITI

Goddess of Boundless Light

As the ancient deity of the primordial vastness of space, the Hindu goddess Aditi is said to have existed before time itself. She is the supreme creator. Called Earth or Dharani, meaning "she who bears," Aditi is the mother of all heavenly bodies, deities, plants and animals. Aditi is also the poetic name of the cow whose milk nourishes all humankind, as evidenced in the continuing worship of sacred cows in India.

As the feminine embodiment of infinity and the cosmos, Aditi defies measurement. She is the endless sky, and she produced offspring called the Adityas, the deities who ruled all aspects of the natural world.

GAURI

Golden Sky Virgin

This Hindu deity is often called Brilliant or Yellow, names referring to her power to bring her followers the prosperity and wealth associated with gold. Gauri is the source of the world, and as the Cosmic Cow, she is the symbol of abundance and fertility. She is known by many other names including Varuna, the goddess of golden liquor, and Parvati, who in her dark form is Shiva's consort. Gauri is also a manifestation of the great warrior goddess Durga, who defended the gods by slaughtering the buffalo Mahisa, the chief of the demons. This event is re-enacted throughout India in the annual Dussera Festival, when Durga is honoured for her triumph of good over evil.

The annual spring Gangau festival in Rajastan is dedicated to Gauri, Parvati and Shiva as symbols of immortal love. Women and girls carry flowers and vessels of water as they dance and sing songs to the Goddess. Gauri is also worshipped all over India in August festivals held to arrange marriages and name babies.

Cumulus clouds and sunrise light, 1995.
Gauri, the Golden Sky Virgin, is the Hindu
source of the world.

AMATERASU

Shinto Sun Goddess

*Futami Rocks, near Ise, Japan, 1989. The sun goddess
Amaterasu rises over the husband and wife rocks that
immortalize her divine parents, Izanagi and Izanami,
honoured with the sacred cord and torii gate.*

This most revered deity of the Shinto religion is the
ancestress of the Imperial family of Japan. The soul
of Amaterasu is said to reside in the *yata-no-kagami*, a
sacred octagonal mirror that maintains her presence at
all royal ceremonies. Amaterasu is the highest manifestation of Kuni-no-tokotachi, the unseen spirit of the
universe. At Ise, the most sacred Shinto site, the hand-
hewn wooden shrines are rebuilt every twenty years.
Certain trees here are adorned with the *shimenawa*, the
sacred cord of Amaterasu that honours the resident
kami, or nature spirits. In Shinto belief, trees are
endowed with speech and the echo of the forest is a
manifestation of the life and soul of the tree.

According to ancient stories, Amaterasu was
angered by her brother Susa-no-wo, the storm god,
who was neglecting his duties, so she shut herself away
in a celestial cave, taking the sun with her. The other
deities pleaded for her return, but she ignored their
calls. Finally Ame-no-uzume, the Dread Female of
Heaven, lured Amaterasu out of the cave by dancing
with her genitals exposed and telling lewd jokes. Her
curiosity piqued, Amaterasu returned the sun to her
people, and a plait of straw (the *shimenawa*) was placed
over the entrance to keep her out of the cave. Now the
sun disappears only at night. This myth is re-enacted
annually in the sacred Kagura ceremony, where dancing priestesses show their genitals to ensure the return
of light and warmth to the world. A less ritual version
can be seen in the red light districts of major Japanese
cities, where dancers perform the striptease called the
tokudashi.

IRIS

Messenger of the Great Mother

It is a universal belief that paradise was originally connected to earth by a rainbow. At the culmination of this heavenly pathway, the seven universal colours blend into the whiteness of a bright, blinding beam of light, seen in the haloes of evolved spiritual beings or during transcendent visions.

Mythologies of many cultures envision the First People arriving on this colourful rope linking heaven with earth. Hindu, Mesopotamian and Judaic art portray the seven heavens in the colours of the rainbow, and the Babylonians painted these hues on the seven levels of their stepped temples, called ziggurats. The veils of Salome and Maya and the stoles of Isis represent the rainbow colours of the seven heavens. Freya and Ishtar both wear rainbow necklaces that convey their power and magic. Iris, the classical Greek messenger of the gods and emissary of the Great Mother, Hera, revealed her presence as a rainbow.

In Africa, Ochumare, the rainbow goddess of the Ochun and Dahomey tribes, links goddesses of the earth and the universe. The Bantu Transformer of Clouds was the Queen's sacred rain-making deity, called the Queen's Arch by the Zulu.

In Aboriginal Australia, the rainbow serpent is the creator being of the Dreamtime. Incan myth says the appearance of a rainbow is the evidence that Father Sky has made Mother Earth very happy in their lovemaking. The Hopi creator goddesses, Huruing Wuhti, met on the rainbow bridge that stretched from east to west. The contemporary tale of a pot of gold at the end of the rainbow can be traced to a Celtic myth in which a form of the Holy Grail, a womb symbol, is related to the pots where Mother Moon kept the souls of the dead in her western paradise.

Rainbow at Iguassu Falls, Brazil, 1995. The void between earthly and heavenly paradise is mediated by the rainbow goddess.

TREE OF LIFE

Union of Heaven and Earth

California redwood grove, 1987. The sacred forest is the living symbol of the goddess.

The tree was one of the earliest symbols of the goddess. From the Paleolithic cave where she was worshipped in the form of a stalagmite or stalactite projecting from her earthly womb, to the sacred grove providing sanctuary for her rituals, to the temple containing her sacred pillar or the sanctified trunk draped with offerings, living wood was seen as the life-giving essence of the goddess. Isis and Hathor were both revered as Lady of the Sycamore, the tree that birthed the sun god and harboured the body of Osiris; Cybele was guardian of the pine tree; Hera and Athena carried the sacred fig branch; Asherah's symbol was a living tree; the Virgin Mary was portrayed in a fifth-century Greek poem as the Tree of Brilliant Fruit and in Chartres Cathedral as the Madonna of the Pillar.

Just as the rainbow goddesses connect the earthly and heavenly paradises throughout the cosmic ether, so the World Tree extends its roots deep into the earth and its branches into the heavens. It is our task from the Goddess to remember to stay rooted in the land as we dance within the web of Spider Woman, connecting us to the source and to all living beings, allowing us to explore both the earthly world and the heavenly world in our search for paradise.

Sakura tree in full bloom (computer enhanced), Japan, 1989.
The Tree of Life connects us to our earthly roots and our heavenly
paradise, allowing us to blossom into our wholeness.

Bibliography

GODDESS LITERATURE

Allione, Tsultrim. *Women of Wisdom.* London: Arkana, 1986.

Ann, Martha, and Dorothy Meyers Imel. *Goddesses in World Mythology.* New York: Oxford University Press, 1993.

Austin, Hallie Iglehart. *The Heart of the Goddess,* Berkely, Calif.: Wingbow press, 1990.

Baring, Ann, and Jules Cashford. *The Myth of the Goddess: Evolution of an Image.* London: Arkana, 1991.

Berndt, Ronald. Kunapippi: *A Study of an Australian Aboriginal Religious Cult.* New York: International University Press, 1974.

Beth, Rae. *Lamp of the Goddess: Lives and Teachings of a Priestess.* York Beach, Maine: Samuel Weiser, 1994.

Blair, Nancy. *Amulets of the Goddess.* Oakland, Calif.: Wingbow Press, 1993.

Bolen, Jean Shinoda. *Crossing to Avalon.* San Francisco: HarperSanFrancisco, 1994.

—. *Goddesses in Everywoman.* New York: Harper & Row, 1984.

Castle, Leila, ed. *Earthwalking Sky Dancers: Women's Pilgrimages to Sacred Places.* Berkeley, Calif.: Frog Ltd., 1996.

Christ, Carol. *The Laughter of Aphrodite.* San Francisco: Harper & Row, 1987.

Conway, D. J. *Maiden, Mother, Crone.* St. Paul, Minn.: Llewellyn, 1995.

Downing, Christine. *The Goddess: Mythological Images of the Feminine.* New York: Crossroad Publishing, 1989.

Eisler, Riane. *The Chalice and the Blade.* San Francisco: HarperSanFrancisco, 1988.

Gadon, Elinor. *The Once and Future Goddess: A Symbol for Our Time.* San Francisco: Harper & Row, 1989.

Galland, China. *Longing for Darkness: Tara and the Black Madonna.* New York: Penguin, 1990.

Gimbutas, Marija. *The Language of the Goddess.* San Francisco: HarperSanFrancisco, 1991.

Gottner-Abendroth, Heide. *The Goddess and Her Heroes.* Stow, Mass.: Anthony Publishing, 1995.

Halifax, Joan. *The Fruitful Darkness: Reconnecting with the Body of the Earth.* San Francisco: HarperSanFrancisco, 1993.

Haskins, Susan. *Mary Magdalen: Myth and Metaphor.* New York: Riverhead Books, 1993.

Johnston, Basil. *The Manitous: The Spiritual World of the Ojibway.* Toronto: Key Porter, 1995.

Johnson, Buffie. *Lady of the Beasts: The Goddess and Her Sacred Animals.* Rochester, Vt.: Inner Traditions, 1994.

Jones, Kathy. *The Goddess in Glastonbury.* Glastonbury, UK: Ariadne Publications, 1996.

Kinstler, Clysta. *The Moon Under Her Feet.* San Francisco: HarperSanFrancisco, 1991.

Lambert, Johanna, ed. *Wise Women of the Dreamtime: Aboriginal Tales of the Ancestral Powers.* Rochester, Vt.: Inner Traditions, 1993.

Larrington, Carolyne, ed. *The Feminist Companion to Mythology.* London: HarperCollins, Pandora Press, 1992.

Leeming, David, and Jake Page. *Goddess: Myths of the Female Divine.* New York: Oxford University Press, 1994.

Mann, A.T., and Jane Lyle. *Sacred Sexuality.* Shaftesbury, UK: Element, 1995.

Matthews, Caitlin. *The Elements of the Goddess.* Shaftesbury, UK: Element, 1989.

—. *Sophia: Goddess of Wisdom.* London: HarperCollins, 1992.

Monaghan, Patricia. *The Book of Goddesses and Heroines.* New York: E.P. Dutton; St. Paul, Minn.: Llewellyn, 1993.

—. *O Mother Sun! A New View of the Cosmic Feminine.* Freedom, Calif.: Crossing Press, 1994.

Mortifee, Ann. *Healing Journey.* Jabula Records (Vancouver), CD, 1994.

Omifunke. "Keys to Feminine Empowerment." (Unpublished manuscript.) http://www.voiceofwomen.com/omi.html.

Plaskow, Judith, and Carol P. Christ. *Weaving the Visions: Patterns in Feminist Spirituality.* San Francisco: Harper & Row, 1989.

Pollack, Rachel. *The Body of the Goddess.* Rockport, Mass.: Element, 1997.

Poth, Dee. *The Goddess Speaks: Myths and Meditations.* Portland, Ore.: Sybyl Publications, 1994.

Shaw, Miranda. *Passionate Enlightenment: Women in Tantric Buddhism.* Princeton, N.J.: Princeton University Press, 1994.

Sjoo, Monica, and Barbara Mor. *The Great Cosmic Mother: Rediscovering the Religion of the Earth.* San Francisco: HarperSanFrancisco, 1987.

Sours, Michael W. "The Maid of Heaven, the Image of Sophia, and the Logos: Personification of the Spirit of God in Scripture and Sacred Literature." Journal of Baha'i Studies (4.1.1991): 46–65.

Starck, Marcia, and Gynne Stern. *The Dark Goddess: Dancing with the Shadow.* Freedom, Calif.: Crossing Press, 1993.

Starhawk. *The Fifth Sacred Thing.* New York: Bantam, 1993.

—. *The Spiral Dance: A Rebirth of the Ancient Religion of the Great Goddess.* San Francisco: HarperSanFrancisco, 1979, 1989.

Stone, Merlin. *Ancient Mirrors of Womanhood*. Boston: Beacon Press, 1990.

—. *When God Was a Woman*. New York: Harcourt Brace, 1976.

Straffon, Cheryl. *Pagan Cornwall: Land of the Goddess*. Penzance, UK: Meyn Mamvro Publications, 1993.

Streep, Peg. *Sanctuaries of the Goddess*. New York: Little, Brown, Bulfinch Press, 1994.

Waldherr, Kris. *The Book of Goddesses*. Hillsboro, Ore.: Beyond Words Publishing, 1995.

Walker, Barbara. *The Woman's Encyclopedia of Myths and Secrets*. San Francisco: HarperSanFrancisco, 1983.

Ward, Tim. *Arousing the Goddess*. Toronto: Somerville House, 1996.

Woodman, Marion. "The Role of the Feminine in the New Era." *Journal of Baha'i Studies* (2.1.1989): 59–65.

Woodman, Marion, and Elinor Dickson. *Dancing in the Flames: The Dark Goddess in the Transformation of Consciousness*. Toronto: Knopf; Boston: Shambhala, 1996.

Woodman, Ross. "The Role of the Feminine in the Baha'i Faith." *Journal of Baha'i Studies* (7.2.1995): 75–97.

Woolger, Jennifer Barker, and Roger J. Woolger. *The Goddess Within*. New York: Ballantine Books, 1987.

GENERAL

Anand, Margo. *The Art of Sexual Ecstasy*. New York: Jeremy Tarcher/Perigee, 1989.

—. *The Art of Sexual Magic*. New York: Jeremy Tarcher/Putnam, 1995.

Artress, Lauren. *Walking a Sacred Path: Rediscovering the Labyrinth as a Spiritual Tool*. New York: Riverhead Books, 1995.

Best, Elsdon. "Maori Religion and Mythology." *Dominion Museum Bulletin*, Wellington, New Zealand, 1982.

Bierhorst, John. *The Mythology of Mexico and Central America*. New York: William Morrow, 1990.

—. *The Mythology of North America*. New York: William Morrow, 1985.

—. *The Mythology of South America*. New York: William Morrow, 1988.

Breeden, Stanley, and Belinda Wright. *Kakadu: Looking After the Country the Gagudju Way*. East Roseville, Australia: Simon & Schuster, 1989.

Brightman, Robert A. *Acaoohkiwina and Acimowina: Traditional Narratives of the Rock Cree Indians*. Canadian Museum of Civilization, Mercury Series Paper 113. Hull, Que., 1989.

Brown, Jennifer S. H., and Robert Brightman. *The Orders of the Dreamed: George Nelson on Cree and Northern Ojibwa Religion and Myth, 1823*. Winnipeg: University of Manitoba Press, 1988.

Childress, David Hatcher. *Lost Cities and Ancient Mysteries of South America*. Stelle, Ill.: Adventures Unlimited Press, 1986.

Cotterell, Arthur. *Classical Mythology*. London: Ultimate Editions, 1997.

Dames, Michael. *Mythic Ireland*. London: Thames and Hudson, 1996.

Dixon, Roland. *Mythology of All Races*. Vol. 9. New York: Marshall Jones, 1916.

Drewek, Paula A. "Feminine Forms of the Divine in Baha'i Scriptures." *Journal of Baha'i Studies* (5.1.1992): 13–23.

Gold, Peter. *Navajo and Tibetan Sacred Wisdom: The Circle of the Spirit*. Rochester, Vt.: Inner Traditions, 1994.

Hackin, J., et al. *Asiatic Mythology*. New York: Crown, Crescent Books, 1993.

Hamilton, Edith. *Mythology: Timeless Tales of Gods and Heroes*. New York: Meridian, 1940, 1969.

Heinberg, Richard. *Memories and Visions of Paradise: Exploring the Universal Myth of a Lost Golden Age*. Los Angeles: Jeremy Tarcher, 1989.

Jordan, Michael. *Encyclopedia of Gods*. New York: Facts on File, 1993.

Kenyatta, Jomo. *Facing Mount Kenya*. Nairobi: Heinemann Educational, 1938.

Leeming, David Adams. *The World of Myth*. New York: Oxford University Press, 1990.

Martin, Henno. *The Sheltering Desert*. Parklands, South Africa: Donkers, 1983.

Miller, Sherrill. *The Pilgrim's Guide to the Sacred Earth*. Toronto: Penguin, 1992.

Milne, Courtney. *The Sacred Earth*. Toronto: Penguin, 1992; New York: Abrams, 1993.

—. *Sacred Places in North America: A Journey into the Medicine Wheel*. New York: Stewart, Tabori & Chang, 1995.

—. *Spirit of the Land*. Toronto: Penguin, 1994.

Moore, Thomas. *Care of the Soul*. New York: HarperCollins, 1992.

Poignant, Roslyn. *Oceanic Mythology: The Myths of Polynesia, Micronesia, Melanesia, Australia*. London: Paul Hamlyn, 1967.

Reed, A. W. *Aboriginal Myths: Tales of the Dreamtime*. Frenchs Forest, Australia: Reed Books, 1978.

Ross, Anne. *Pagan Celtic Britain*. London: Constable, 1992.

Scully, Vincent. *The Earth, the Temple, and the Gods*. Newhaven, Ct.: Yale University Press, 1962.

Senior, Michael. *Illustrated Who's Who in Mythology*. London: McDonald & Co., 1985.

Swain, Tony, and Gary Trompf. *Religions of Oceania*. Library of Religious Beliefs and Practices. London: Routledge, 1995.

van der Post, Laurens. *The Heart of the Hunter*. London: Penguin, 1965.

Vardey, Lucinda, ed. *God in All Worlds*. Toronto: Knopf, 1995.

Willis, Roy, ed. *World Mythology*. New York: Henry Holt, 1993.

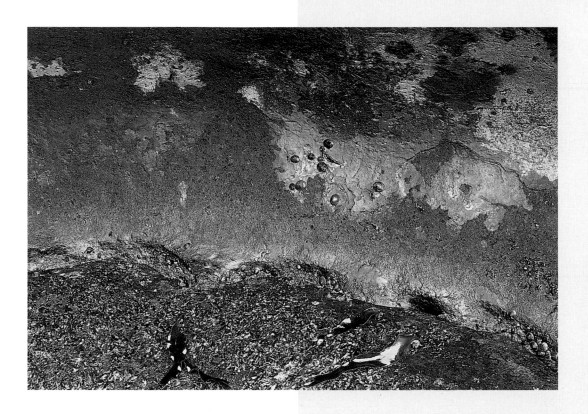

Detail of sea cave, west coast of Vancouver Island, 1996.

This book is set in ITC Golden Cockerel, a typeface originally designed in 1929 by Eric Gill, a sculptor and wood-engraver. The type was commissioned by Golden Cockerel Press to be used in a special edition of the *Four Gospels*. This was the first of Gill's typeface designs that he supervised through the entire metal-type manufacturing process. Some claim that it is one of the best versions ever made of a Renaissance face for use in modern times.